THE GUIDE SHOOTS FIRST

THE GUIDE SHOOTS FIRST

WILLIAM D. BAKER

FIRST EDITION • June 2010

14 13 12 11 10   1 2 3 4 5

2010928522

ISBN 13: 978-0-9821405-2-9
ISBN 10: 0-9821405-2-5

Manufactured in the United States of America.
Designed by James Monroe Design, LLC.

For information about special purchases or custom editions, please contact:

James Monroe Publishing, LLC.
A Division of James Monroe Design, LLC.
7236 Bald Eagle Lane
Willow River, Minnesota 55795

www.jamesmonroedesign.com

To my friends in Dickey County, North Dakota,
and the memory of two fine sportsmen,
Bob Van Hauer and Tom Reed.

French Proverb

There are no hunted, there are no hunters,
there is only the hunt.

CONTENTS

SIX

SEVEN

EIGHT

NINE

TEN

ELEVEN

TWELVE

ACKNOWLEDGEMENTS

The drawings at the beginnings of six chapters in this book are the work of Paula Romo of Bedford, Texas. Paula works full-time in Dallas, attends college in the evenings, and in her limited spare time does freelance art work. She is a petite, talented, young lady who was able to listen to my verbal descriptions of various events and somehow transfer them to paper in a humourous yet empathetic format.

My favorite student at Concordia College in Moorhead, Minnesota, Elizabeth Eickhoff, did all the manuscript typing. While her typing skills are excellent, it is Beth's ability to decipher my writing and the accompaning arrows and crossouts, that makes her so valuable to the process. Her good sense, coupled with uncommon intuition, brings order out of chaos.

I must also offer my thanks to all my friends who agreed, without hesitation, to permit me to use their real names in telling these stories. They all acquiesed without knowing how they were going to be depicted. Such trust is heartwarming.

INTRODUCTION

I have long been encouraged to document some of the more memorable events of my outdoor life and the characters that were involved in those events. These are the vivid vignettes I have recounted to my family and friends many times. Some are humorous, some involve pathos, some are illuminating, some resulted in hospital confinement, and some just portray the human condition.

With two exceptions, they all involved some type of hunting activity, an endeavor as old as mankind, but in the case of my generation, not necessary for survival. Instead, it represents a primordial, fundamental relief from the artificial. It is a return to the fresh air, sunrises, and sunsets of the North American prairie; an opportunity to witness the grain harvests and the metronomic rhythm of the annual migrations. There is absolutely nothing like standing alone on a wind-filled expanse of prairie with the sky a blue bowl above you to make you aware of your Lilliputian stature and insignificance, at the same time grasping an awareness of the grandeur of this planet and the gift of life.

This is akin to a religious experience and very good for your soul. I look forward each year to this revitalization, and I cherish the memories of the last forty-five years.

ONE

DICKEY COUNTY

In the fall of 1965, my hunting partner, Bob Van Hauer, and I were driving his Chevrolet Carryall, packed with hunting gear, including a substantial tent, through south-eastern North Dakota on our way to Saskatchewan, Canada, to hunt ducks. This was prior to Interstate 94 being constructed, so we were traveling the blue high-ways. As we both lived in Golden Valley, Minnesota, our nearest escape route to the northwest was the vener-able Floyd B. Olson Memorial Highway, also known as Minnesota State Highway 55. At the North Dakota border this ribbon of asphalt transformed itself into North Dakota State Highway 11, and we continued to motor on west along that route, just a few miles north of the South Dakota line. It was, and still is, a sparsely traveled road.

Our intention was to stay on Highway 11 another two hundred miles, turn north at the Missouri River to Bismarck, then on to Minot and then into Canada. We had no specific destination in Saskatchewan; we would just wander around until we saw thousands of ducks in the air and set up camp. So are great journeys of exploration launched. First the idea is conceived, then shared, then lift-off. By definition, great journeys of exploration don't require a specific destination, unless you're going to the Moon or Mars, or one of the poles.

In some respects, Van and I were an odd couple. He was twenty years my senior; having been born in 1910, he was a widower with six children, a devout Catholic, had been a captain in the Army in World War II, held a master's degree in economics, and earned his living as a hospital administrator. I, on the other hand, was a married father of four, a relaxed Methodist, had attained the estimable rank of corporal during my post-war stint in the U.S. Air Force, and had a bachelor's degree in zoology, which naturally qualified me to become an insurance broker. We were, however, simpatico or synoptic in that we viewed the world in the same way. Van was raised in central Montana and I in central South Dakota, engendering a common love and understanding of the great outdoors. We both excelled in school and worked our way through college, resulting in a mind-set that bordered on stubbornness but which we viewed as goal-oriented. We each considered problems not necessarily as opportunities in every instance, but as obstacles to be overcome. Even if it required years of effort, or as it sometimes happens given enough time, the problem becomes irrelevant.

Some two hours into the North Dakota segment of our drive we entered Dickey County and started to notice that the potholes contained more ducks than we had previously seen in Minnesota. We were entering the eastern edge of the prairie pothole area encompassing the Dakotas and Saskatchewan, the premier breeding ground in North America for ducks: a veritable duck factory. As sunset was only an hour away, large skeins of geese were also moving out to feed, and cock pheasants were shimmering in the late sun at the edges of the cornfields.

Considering that we had traveled three hundred miles that day from Minneapolis, leaving us with another five hundred miles to our destination, and that we were under the time restraints of a one-week vacation from the office, stopping to hunt in Dickey County would afford us five days of pleasurable hunting versus three days in Canada. I can't remember which one of us first verbalized that thought, but like most of our ideas the other bought in quickly.

That was another characteristic we shared: a propensity to decide quickly if we saw what appeared to be an opportunity. As we viewed the world through a common prism, we were each perhaps a touch too eager to second the other's motion. Over the years this led to several outdoor blunders that negated otherwise thoughtful plans to apprehend our feathered friends. With little regard for the consequences, but in an attempt to further our sons' education, we shared these errors with our boys, much to their amusement. They in turn shared the stories of our exploits with everyone in camp, and with the retellings, legends involving parental ineptitude were created. I'm very pleased to say that both of my sons, as well as Van's middle son, Jan, have now committed their own share of gaffes, so I no longer have to suffer these outrageous allegations.

After deciding to throw out our anchor in Dickey County, the next question was, where? As the county encompassed 11,520 square miles that were sparsely settled, the possibilities of where to pitch our sixty-four-square-foot tent were almost limitless, but trespassing was not in our nature. We needed permission from a willing and understanding landowner. I did have a tenuous connection with two Dickey County residents, Earl Larson and his wife Eldora. Let me elaborate on that tenuousness. The Larsons' daughter was married to the son of a fellow who worked for me in Minneapolis. I had met the Larsons at their daughter's wedding, and I recalled they lived near Oakes, which is the largest town in Dickey County. They were listed in the telephone book, and when I called they actually remembered meeting me and invited us to their home for dinner. Their farm was located fourteen miles due west of Oakes on a paved road and adjacent to the Maple River, a sometimes flowing stream perhaps ten feet in width, substantial for North Dakota.

Not only did the hospitable Larsons provide us with an excellent home-cooked meal, but Earl also suggested we set up our camp on their land next to the river. We got the impression that having two hunters camping on their property would give them something a bit out of the ordinary to discuss with their neighbors, but primarily the invitation was extended out of their kindness and generosity. It was a first-rate campsite with water handy and some shelter from the wind provided by their neighbor Buzz Gramlow's shelterbelt, a mature growth of trees planted in the mid-1930s.

I mentioned that our tent, which was actually my tent (Van referred to it as *The Baker Tent*) was substantial. The thick canvas alone weighed close to two hundred pounds and required two strong men to lift it out of the Carryall. The wooden poles, heavy ropes, and metal stakes added another hundred pounds or so, and it was the ideal shelter to erect on the blustery North Dakota prairie. I wonder now whatever became of that tent. Measuring only eight feet by eight feet, with a front flap that could be elevated on poles to serve as a portico and give us more area under canvas, it reveled in the constant wind. It was in its element.

Unfortunately, the following winter Van was smitten by the appearance of a much larger but lighter and less bulky tent that was on display in Dayton's department store. It was secured to a metal frame that was erected outside of the canvas, so the tent in fact hung from the frame. It looked quite elegant situated on the fourth floor of Dayton's, an area not known for its wind. He put down his money, took the tent home, and the next fall, in October of 1966, we transported the shiny new tent to our campsite in North Dakota.

Returning to the spot between the Maple River and the shelterbelt, we erected Van's proud purchase in short order and wandered down the river for a quick reconnaissance. Returning in an hour we noticed the wind had twisted the metal frame supporting the tent to a considerable degree. It resembled a bizarre, modern-art sculpture designed by a bipolar artist in the grip of depression. A few minutes spent reworking the frame and some extra tie-downs returned the shelter to its original form, although I for one expressed concern about its durability.

The tent did survive the night, albeit with considerable groaning and flapping. We were gone from camp most of the next day, spooking geese with great enthusiasm but little success, which marked our early attempts to think like a goose. Returning to our home by the river at late dusk we were most disappointed to find the tent twisted in a more bizarre shape than yesterday. Obviously, the manic side of our artist friend had conquered his depression, the result resembling a shower curtain intertwined with metal rods and neatly wrapped in bits of rope. We slept in the truck that night.

The same drill continued for the balance of the week. Every morning we reworked and re-erected *Van's Tent* and, after a tiring day in the fields, we returned in the evening to chaos. That flimsy creature simply could not withstand the elements. It really belonged on the fourth floor of Dayton's. Finally, on our last day, we returned to an empty campsite. The tent was gone. It had disappeared. We looked along the riverbank in both directions to no avail. Stopping at the Larson farm on our way to dinner at Ruby's Café in Fullerton, we inquired of Earl if he had seen the tent.

"Yes," he replied, "I was picking corn this afternoon, and it went by me at considerable speed, rolled up in a ball, and it looked like it was headed for Oakes."

Over the following winter months Van set out to solve our outdoor-housing problem utilizing his inherent Dutch ingenuity. He resolved to stay out of department stores and build his own structure. The result was an eight-by-twelve-foot pre-fab Quonset hut with plywood walls, a door, a floor, and a canvas roof supported by wooden rafters that ran the length of the building. Over time he assembled it in his driveway, then disassembled it and packed it on a flatbed trailer, ready to go to North Dakota.

In October of 1967 we set out on what had now become our annual expedition to Dickey County, this time hauling Van's latest experiment behind the Carryall and my son Billy, age nine, in the backseat with Van's dog, Taffy, and my black Lab, Mandy. Billy represented the second generation of Bakers to visit Dickey County and the beginning of the tradition "You can't go hunting until you're nine years of age," which all the grandsons honor to this day, while their mothers lobby to increase the minimum age to ten or eleven.

The plywood structure was wind-resistant, and although Van had thoughtfully provided flooring, for some reason it was very cold inside. His elaborate construction planning had neglected an allowance for insulation. Unfortunately, that weekend in North Dakota the temperature plummeted, the potholes froze, and so did we. Even fully dressed and tucked into our sleeping bags, we chattered and shivered through the night. I once tried to entice Mandy into my sleeping bag and might have succeeded if I hadn't caught her tail in the zipper. The cold didn't seem to bother Billy, but Van and I were most uncomfortable.

On Saturday night, our third and last night in camp,

the inside thermometer registered eighteen degrees Fahrenheit. Suddenly we heard a knock on the door, and Dick Sturma, the manager of the Fullerton Farmers Elevator, entered our icebox.

"My wife says the boy should come home with me. It's much too cold for him to be outside on a night like this."

It was obvious he was reluctant to suggest anything approaching child abuse, but it was equally obvious that Frances Sturma had told him not to come back without Billy in tow. My duty as a father required that I acquiesce, and I was about to do so when Van piped up in a plaintive tone, "What about us?"

Sturma hadn't anticipated this response and had no instructions except for my son's rescue. We could see the wheels turning.

"Okay, you can all sleep in the office at the elevator. The heat is on there."

Now Van was pushing his luck. "What about the dogs?"

Dick's initial reaction was to deny access to our four-legged friends, but as you all know there is no canine capable of a more woebegone, dejected look than a Labrador retriever. One glance at poor Mandy and her damaged tail was all it took.

"Okay. Bring the dogs, too."

We were a happy bunch of campers when we left that camp. We bedded down on the floor of the warm elevator office and were so glad we had invited Billy on this trip. He accepted his role as our savior with the aplomb and the circumspection of a nine-year-old boy and maintains to this day that the rescue was unnecessary, as he wasn't cold. I cautioned him, "Don't ever tell that to Mrs. Sturma."

TWO

FULLERTON

The nearest village to the Larson farm and our camp was Fullerton, located a mile west and another mile north or, as the locals say, "One west and one north." Fullerton was your quintessential small North Dakota farming community. When we first arrived there it contained Glynn's grocery store, Ruby's Café, a bank that had been converted into a bar owned by B. C. Simek, Mark's

Standard Station, a high school, the Farmers Elevator, a Catholic church, two Protestant churches—both served by the same pastor but with Sunday services an hour apart—a post office, and the Dickey Rural Telephone Company. This infrastructure served a population of maybe one hundred residents in the town and another two hundred people on the surrounding farms. The dominant structures were the ever-expanding grain elevator and an old railroad hotel serving as a private residence across from the grain elevator and adjacent to the Soo Line tracks. Fullerton was a weather-beaten, dusty, unglamorous place that appeared to be hanging on to the twentieth century by its fingernails.

Sixty years earlier the population had been closer to five hundred and the local businesses included the Carroll House Hotel, the Kingsby Store, the Jay Stiles Store, the Fullerton State Bank, a land office for Mr. Sweet and his attorney, Benjamin Porter, the Fullerton Lumber Company, a hardware store, a café, and a meat market. There were only the two Protestant churches at that time; St. Patrick's Catholic Church didn't exist until the 1920s.

The town had been founded in 1887 by E. P. Fuller and his son-in-law Edwin Sweet. Mr. Sweet, at the time a thirty-year-old graduate of Yale University and the University of Michigan School of Law, was apparently a young man of some energy and vision. He married Sophia Fuller in 1876, practiced law in Grand Rapids, Michigan, and was elected mayor of that fine city. In 1880 he and his father-in-law acquired 1,200 acres of land in central Dickey County, Dakota Territory. An additional quarter section of land was acquired in 1895 under the Homestead Act, but not for homesteading, but for *timber culture,* which must have been Congress's way of atoning for permitting all of the trees in Minnesota and Wisconsin to be harvested. Like many well-intended acts of Congress gone awry, it failed to understand that the prairie, with its limited rainfall, was not the ideal environment for establishing a forest.

In 1882 Mr. Sweet traveled to Dickey County to inspect their holdings and hopefully to establish a town site. After surveying and plotting a town, he named it Fullerton in honor of his partner and father-in-law. In 1887 he signed an agreement with the Minneapolis, St. Paul and Sault St. Marie Railroad (Soo Line), which was building westward from Minneapolis to Bismarck, to lay tracks through Fullerton in exchange for free right-of-way and the building of a depot. They began selling lots, and Fullerton was on its way. Sweet also donated land for a school, a church, a cemetery, and a park. Situated in the geographical center of Dickey County, it was thought to be ideal for the county seat, but that was not to be the case. Ellendale, as the first settlement in the county, secured that honor in 1889 when Dakota Territory was divided along the 46th parallel into the two new states of North and South Dakota.

Mr. Sweet, in keeping with his entrepreneurial nature, in 1888 commissioned a Mr. Burchard, a building contractor from Michigan, to build a three-story hotel adjacent to the Soo Line tracks. A local carpenter, Herman Keller, was hired to help. The hotel, with its fancy French mansard-style architecture, looked "elegant but strange" to the locals when completed in 1889. While there were hundreds of railroad hotels built in the Dakotas in the closing decades of the nineteenth century, it certainly was one of the few hotels on the prairie that could boast of a *ballroom* on the third floor.

The *Ellendale Leader*, on December 7, 1888, wrote "Ground has been broken for a hotel 40' by 60' in Fullerton. It will have three stories with a Mansard roof. This roof will be the most distinguishing feature of the building." So the building was the only hotel on the prairie with a ballroom *and* a mansard roof.

The hotel, which was christened the Carroll House after Mr. Sweet's oldest son Carroll, was the center of social life in Dickey County in the late nineteenth and early twentieth centuries. When we first arrived in Fullerton, in 1965, it was owned and occupied by Robert (Rob) Johnson, who had purchased the building in 1944 from Mr. Sweet's daughter, Sophia Sweet Janeway, for $325. I visited with Rob several times during our trips to Fullerton. He was a bright man, artistic, very interested in North Dakota history, and an inveterate collector of anything relating to that history. Every room in the Carroll House was crowded with the fruits of his collecting obsession. Books, newspapers, jars, prizewinning ears of corn, arrowheads, pictures, and the gun purported to have killed the last buffalo in Dickey County, that incident having taken place just southwest of Fullerton in March of 1883.

The business of North Dakota is agriculture, and that applies in spades to the six townships surrounding Fullerton. At the core of that business, with some notable exceptions, is the family farm. When land became available in Dickey County in the early 1880s, settlers from the East flocked to the quarter- and half-section tracts available at little or no cost. By the terms of the Homestead Act of 1862, settlers could acquire their land by living on it and farming for five years, or they could simply buy it outright for $1.25 per acre.

When the Soo Line Railroad pushed its tracks into Fullerton in 1887, transportation of the settlers' wheat harvest to the giant flour mills in Minneapolis became possible, and grain elevators to store the crops sprung up adjacent to the railway. Fullerton's first elevator, the Atlantic, was built in 1887. A few years later a second elevator, the Minnetonka, was added and later a third, the Marshall-McCartney.

Through the years these structures were altered and

rebuilt and finally merged in 1919 into the Fullerton Equity Elevator Company, a farmer-owned and controlled entity that is the economic engine for the surrounding areas. It is known today as the Fullerton Farmers Elevator, and its many structures, stretching over three-quarters of a mile, dominate the skyline of Fullerton. Of course, anything taller than two stories would dominate the skyline of Fullerton. The total storage capacity of this behemoth is 3.5 million bushels, and the total volume processed each year is about 14 million bushels, mostly corn and soybeans. This ranks it among the top five percent of all the elevators in North Dakota. It is a BIG business that includes the sale of seed, feed, chemicals, and fertilizer. Genial Andy Hager runs this operation but is never too busy to chat with visitors and share his stock of Fullerton Farmers Elevator caps.

Some four miles to the south of Fullerton is the Maple River Hutterite Colony. It was established in 1961, just a few years before Van and I wandered into Dickey County. The members of the colony follow the teachings of Jakob Hutter, who was born and raised in South Tyrol, which is today part of Italy. He was by trade a hatmaker—hence the German name *Hutter* (Hatter). He was elected the leader of a group of Anabaptists, a sect made up primarily of peasants and artisans who wanted economic and political reform in addition to the religious changes proposed by Martin Luther at that time. Needless to say the reforms preached by the Anabaptists were extremely threatening to the established social order, so their persecution was ruthless. Hutter organized a congregation in nearby Austria, thereby attracting the attention of the Catholic Church, and in 1536 he was captured by the Jesuits and burned at the stake at Innsbruck.

The Hutterites are similar to the Amish and the Mennonites, who also trace their roots to the Radical Reformation in the sixteenth century. Their philosophy is to live simply, share everything, avoid Jesuits at all cost, and trust in God. These precepts combined with absolute pacifism have naturally subjected them to persecution over the centuries and forced them to wander through many different European countries. They came to North America from the Ukraine in the late nineteenth century and are scattered down the center of the continent from Canada all the way into Mexico. Their original settlements were in southeast South Dakota, and I have been aware of the sect since my childhood without ever learning much about them. Their U.S. population has grown over the past 125 years from four hundred to over fifty thousand, all living in communes in distinctly rural areas. Among themselves, they speak a Germanic dialect which originated in Southern Austria and has a number of loan words from Slavic languages and English.

The 150 or so Hutterites now residing in the Maple River Colony were spun off from a colony in Saskatchewan,

Canada. They immigrated down to North Dakota and started buying land south of Fullerton in the early 1960s. Although it's a closely guarded secret, as it is with most landowners in the Dakotas, I would estimate they now own or rent 7,000 to 8,000 acres and are excellent farmers. The colony also produces structural steel products in a small but growing factory and raises thousands of geese. Everyone in the group sleeps on goose-down pillows and under goose-down quilts, as do I as a regular buyer of these products. The families live in their own individual houses, complete with sidewalks, but take all their meals together in the dining hall. Well, not completely together, as the women eat at one table and the men at another. The children also have their own table. The ladies prefer not to eat with the men because the men eat too fast and then return immediately to the fields, while the gals like to enjoy a more leisurely mealtime and chat a bit before returning to work.

Everyone over the age of seven works in the colony. There is, of course, no television, that device being accurately portrayed as an instrument of the devil. In the best examples of where their priorities lay, however, the Hutterites do enjoy the most modern of agricultural and culinary equipment. In all my travels I have never seen a cleaner, larger, or better-equipped kitchen. This is obviously necessary when you are serving three meals a day, 365 days a year, to 150 people. On a recent tour of their kitchen I was most impressed by an automatic shelving device in the walk-in cooler. Just push a button and the shelves revolve until the required product appcars.

One of my more memorable visits to the Colony took place in the mid-70s when I convinced two teenage boys, Scott Baker and Kenny Carlson, that accompanying me would advance their education. Of course I didn't suggest that uninteresting possibility to them, but rather said that we might get something to eat from the good ladies. My long-term memory is excellent, but for some reason I can't recall my rationale for visiting the colony at that time. I do remember asking to see the Head Lady, who was the wife of the Head Guy, so I may have been looking for someone to clean ducks.

Whenever I had arrived alone, my presence hadn't created much of a stir. The inhabitants who might glance at me quickly returned to their business. However, this time, when my two healthy and attractive young acolytes emerged from the vehicle behind me, something very unusual occurred. Some mysterious telepathic signal had evidently been transmitted, and a substantial percentage of females in the colony piled out of their houses, the Head Lady in the lead. The appearance of, shall I say, a crowd of curious females of all ages, but with one obvious common estrogen-driven motive, was disconcerting to me and downright frightening to the boys. They stepped closely behind me, attempting to occupy the same space as I.

You must understand that one of the major problems facing any insular group is the necessarily small gene pool that exists. From the way these gals were inspecting my young friends they had already passed most if not all of their qualifying genetic tests. The boys intuitively understood the primeval vibrations emanating from the crowd and wanted no part of it. It took several decades of absence for the memory of that experience to wane enough for either Scott or Kenny to set foot in the settlement again.

My current best friend at the colony is Annie Waldner, a seventy-eight-year-old widow to whom I pay my respects on every visit to Dickey County. Annie is an energetic little lady whose great joy in life is selling me homemade pillows, slippers, and dishtowels. Over the years I have acquired more than enough of this stuff, but with each visit I seem to come away with more, plus another free bottle of her homemade elderberry wine, which is actually quite good, especially if you ignore the container, a Jim Beam whiskey bottle. Very eclectic marketing. She also enjoys giving me an annual kitchen tour.

The center for social life in Fullerton today is the Ranch House, a combination bar and restaurant now owned by a nonprofit corporation which was funded by some of the local citizens. It is managed by Geraldine Glynn, a personable yet businesslike lady with great multitasking skills. I have witnessed the evolution of the Ranch House from its humble beginnings as Bee's Bar, with sawdust and peanut shells on the floor, to its present supper-club status, serving 150 people for Saturday-night dinner.

The décor of the place is classic Western. The dining room is decorated with Mexican fringed blankets hanging from the corner rafters and wall decorations made of wheat and assorted grasses. Over the swinging doors leading into the kitchen is a WELCOME sign made of horseshoes. The welcome sign is in direct opposition to two signs on the two doors below that read EMPLOYEES ONLY. Obviously patrons are welcome in the dining room, but not in the kitchen. Makes sense.

The L-shaped bar has room for a dozen or so stools and standing room for the latecomers. The north wall holds an enormous moose head and an adequate whitetail deer mount. An elk head on the east wall gives some balance to the room. The pole rafters are festooned with the same fringed Mexican blankets as in the dining room. Interspersed below the hunting trophies are various barbed-wire exhibits, waterfowl paintings, beer ads, an American flag, and wrench replicas made of wood. A pull-tab machine sits in one corner of the bar and a popcorn maker in the other.

Of course, the décor becomes secondary when the crowd starts to arrive on a Saturday night and the social interaction begins. Families gather at large tables in the dining room and the regulars on their regular stools at the bar. The out-of-state hunters congregate at the television high on the wall above the bank vault that identifies the joint's more dignified former life as a bank. When I was last there we watched the high-priced Yankees sneak by the hapless Minnesota Twins once again. The noise level is for the most part a calming buzz broken from time to time by shouts and groans from the TV watchers. A pleasant time is always had by all.

THREE

THE CARROLL HOUSE

When Rob Johnson died in the spring of 1969, the news was conveyed to me by Earl Larson, along with the information that Rob's sister and brother, Della and Frank, were the executors of his estate. Upon writing to Frank I learned they would, in fact, be selling the Carroll House in the summer. In the letter that follows he informed me that most of the contents were being gifted to the North

Dakota Historical Society, and Rob's personal effects would be sold, as would the structure itself. Included in the sale would be a sometimes-functioning oil burner in the living room and a small refrigerator.

Fullerton, N.D.
June 2 - '69

Friend William -

We are having a sale next Sat. on Roberts personal property, the hotel is not included though we can except bids. I talked to the lawyer this morning & he said it was O.K to go ahead & sell & from there the courts will take over it is a little more than I understand as it is my first experience of this kind.

The oil stove is hooked up & the oil tank outside, there is also a refrigerator in there and they are going with the hotel if we sell. We are not selling them at the sale.

This is a little sudden notice for you but it is the best we can do.

Sincerely
Frank Johnson (Admr)

(Not necessary that you are here for Sat.)

As I was scheduled to attend the dedication of one of Van's new hospitals, Dakota Midland, in Aberdeen, South Dakota, in August of that year, I arranged to leave a day early and met with Della Johnson in Fullerton. We sat on the front porch of the Carroll House and conducted a transaction that took no more than fifteen minutes. While Della may not have secured the highest bid available she did accept the first cash offer. I'm certain there were locals who would have bid on acquiring the property, but as the harvest was about to commence, they were busy with other things and I slipped in under the radar. Upon learning from Della that Rob had insured the Carroll House for $2,000, I offered her that logical amount. She accepted, and I continued my journey to the dedication in Aberdeen, the proud owner of an eighty-year-old wooden building in dire need of repair, with no plumbing or heating, dangerous lighting, located three hundred miles from my home, that I would only be able to use maybe two weekends a year.

It all made perfect sense until I tried to explain the transaction to my wife, who pointed out that for $2,000 I could stay in the finest motel in Oakes, a place with running water, heat, and maid service, for fifty nights. Or the equivalent of twenty-five weekends, which should take care of my hunting needs for the next twelve years. Obviously, I needed someone to share in the capital expenditure. And who more qualified and more able than my hunting partner, Robert Van Hauer, Esquire?

Van was an easier sell than Della, although I didn't mention the motel alternative. Some things people need to figure out for themselves. So, with my friends at Dorsey handling the legal work, on August 16, 1969, a deed for the Carroll House was issued to William D. Baker and Robert Van Hauer, Tenants in Common. Our residence problems in Dickey County were solved, and while it wasn't as economical as a motel, it was closer to the action and had much more ambiance.

Part of the Carroll House experience is the five-hour land journey from Minneapolis to Fullerton in mid-October. The fall colors, the crimson sumac, the red and gold of the oaks and maples all punctuate the gradual incline to the northwest. You pass through the lake country of central Minnesota with repeated crossings of the North Fork of the Crow River. Drive up, then down, the tumbling glacial moraines around Lake Minnewaska, near Glenwood, and past the stark white silhouette of the Trinity Lutheran Church on the left that marks the halfway point of the journey just outside of Kensington.

It's a good idea to stop for gas and a quick lunch at Elbow Lake, which is the anglicized version of Flekkefjord Lake. You run parallel to the Soo Line (now Canadian Pacific) tracks, and shortly after you bridge the Pomme de Terre River near Barnett, Minnesota, you cross the imperceptible Continental Divide (North–South) and descend imperceptibly into the basin of the Red River of the north and enter the ultraflat Red River Valley at Wendell, Minnesota. This valley is the lakebed of the glacial Lake Agassiz, which during the melting after the last ice age covered an area greater than the combined area of the present Great Lakes, extended seven hundred miles from north to south, and was two hundred miles wide. The vestigial Red River flows north into Lake Winnipeg, which is the Canadian remnant of Lake Agassiz. Lake of the Woods on the Minnesota/Canada border is another remnant.

You speed by Nashua and Tenney, the tiniest and most westerly of Minnesota hamlets, the enormous piles of harvested sugar beets, and the slippery mud on the road from the trucks carrying the beets. Crossing the usually bone-dry Bois de Sioux River you enter the state of North Dakota. Forty years ago the sign greeting visitors at the state line read, "Welcome to Roughrider Country." As machismo became politically incorrect, the sign was changed to "North Dakota–The Peace Garden State." The sign was modified again a few years back and now reads, innocuously, "Discover the Spirit," which, in keeping with our amorphous culture, means whatever you want it to mean.

The slight rise in elevation just east of Hankinson, North Dakota, marks the western boundary of the Red River Valley and the first of the ninety-degree turns for which the Dakotas are famous. The trees are shorter now and scarcer; you are entering the prairie or Coteau ecosystem of North America that stretches for six hundred miles to the west, four hundred miles to the north, and a thousand miles to the south. The only local variations in the landscape are the Tewaukan Hills in South Dakota, ten miles to the south.

Geographic location in and of itself, even when enhanced by architectural or historical ambiance, doesn't generate the almost visceral nostalgia that memories of people interrelating at that locale can produce. When you combine an unusual venue with people such as the ones who gathered in the living room of the Carroll House on weekends in October, such vivid memories are created that I can recall most of the conversations that occurred there over the past forty years. Such as the political discussion, one evening, with one of the Hutterite farmers who was enamored of the Carter administration and its high interest rates. He was obviously a lender, while I was a borrower at that time paying 12–13% interest. He was the only gent I ever asked to leave the premises.

Or the time in 1982 I introduced Bobby Cline as my father-in-law to another local visitor, Mike Bakkegard. Mike, one of the few Norwegians in the area, had dropped by to pay his respects, and I introduced him to my son Scott, my son-in-law Jim Miller, and on a perverse impulse, Bob Cline as my father-in-law. Bobby was actually two years younger than I, although recent events had aged him to a considerable degree. On the first morning, in the dark, he had stepped into a badger hole and twisted his knee to the extent that he was unable to participate in the hunt. Implicit in our shared doctrine was the understanding that if a minor disability prevented you from maintaining the group's pace they were under no obligation to wait for you or assist you in any manner. How the group would proceed with a major injury would require a great deal more discussion and possibly a vote.

So Bobby sat on the ground by the badger hole and waited for our return—just a short two or three hours, but the cold ground caused him some stiffness. So when he was introduced to Mike Bakkergard a few days later, not only did he have a definite limp from his injured knee, but he also was bent over about thirty degrees. This wizened appearance was accented by a three-day growth of grayish beard, not unusual in a fifty-year-old male. Mike peered at Bobby intently, and after Bobby limped into the kitchen he whispered to me, "How old is your father-in-law?" I was somewhat taken aback by the question as I hadn't anticipated having to quantify Cline's senescence. Assuming any father-in-law would have to come from a previous generation, I quickly replied, "He is seventy-two."

Mike smiled sweetly and offered, "That's amazing! He doesn't look a day over sixty-five!" It was a most enjoyable moment for Scott, Jim, and me that we cherish to this day. Bobby, as you might expect, still fails to see the humor in the exchange.

In early October of 1969, Van, Tom Reed, and I all converged at the Carroll House to work some plumbing magic and get water inside the building. Rob Johnson had a water spigot coming out of the well on the south side of the building and evidently had brought in water as needed in a bucket. We were more interested in turning on an inside faucet for our water. It took only an hour or so to drill a hole through the wall, attach an elbow to the outside pipe, run a pipe along the baseboard, and voila, we had water in what was to become the kitchen. It was a difficult hour however, because Van and Tom, in true alpha male fashion, disagreed on every aspect of the project while I attempted to arbitrate the disputes. Eventually I gave up and volunteered to drive to Oakes for more plumbing supplies, expecting to return and find one of them dead on the floor. Instead, when I returned they had completed the job and were congratulating each other with glasses of single malt whiskey in their fists rather than the knives I had expected.

And so began a decade-long process of renovation and improvements to our big house on the prairie. The Carroll House contained four good-sized rooms on the ground floor and five bedrooms on the second floor, with the third floor resembling a rabbit warren as the ballroom had been partitioned off into eight or ten small bedrooms on either side of a hallway. We decided to focus on the ground floor, with the number-one priority being indoor plumbing including a sink, shower, and toilet.

Having been constructed in 1888–1889, the building contained lumber with dimensions not seen today. Everything was oversized, with the floorboards measuring 3.5 inches by 7.75 inches versus today's two-by-six-inch planks. The basic structure was more than sound, even if the exterior showed evidence of gradual deterioration. Sawing through those floorboards by hand involved some real effort, with progress measured a millimeter at a time, but we managed to install a bathroom in 1970. We even hung some waterfowl pictures on the walls and a copy of the Magna Carta in the bathroom for the more historically minded of our guests. The place was starting to resemble a motel in Oakes.

We spent little or no money furnishing the place. We scavenged my mother's old couch, which she was donating to the Salvation Army; the beds were lifted from some now-forgotten source; and for the princely sum of $100 I purchased a large table and eight solid oak chairs from the Minneapolis Athletic Club. This set had been in the bar at the club and had become available because of a remodeling project. One Saturday morning my boys and I drove downtown and loaded that heavy table on the top of the station wagon and hauled it to Golden Valley. Several trips later we managed to move the chairs. Getting the set to North Dakota was solved by a chance encounter in Bee's Bar with a friendly grain-truck driver who regularly hauled grain to Minneapolis in his eighteen-wheeler. He offered to bring the furniture to Fullerton on his next return trip. Even my most circumspect neighbors came outside to watch him back that semi-trailer around a curve and uphill into our driveway. We learned early on that no problem was beyond the capabilities of the citizens of Fullerton. When we needed to install a septic system the mayor was there with his backhoe. If the water heater collapsed, Dean Simek was there to install a new one, on a Sunday, no less.

As we spent only six or seven days a year at the Carroll House, and as we hunted on most days, it's difficult, in retrospect, to comprehend how all of our projects were accomplished. Van and I had a joint checking account for the Carroll House requirements, and we included an improvement project in our planning for every trip. By the mid-1970s the place was more habitable, and we felt comfortable about inviting guests other than our sons to join us on our expeditions. With more people involved, communication with the locals greatly expanded, and we started to feel more like a part of the community that initially had viewed us as decidedly eccentric for tenting on the prairie.

To some people I suppose it's progress, but new commercial hunting camps have sprung up in Dickey County, particularly in the Fullerton area, resulting in more land being leased for their purposes. It's unseemly of me, I know, but I am nostalgic about the old days when we were practically the only hunters in the area. We can't complain however; we've had forty great years at the Carroll House and, most importantly, have acquired many good friends in Fullerton over those years.

On the fourteenth day of October in 1981, Van and I signed a Quit Claim Deed transferring the title of the Carroll House to the Fullerton Community Betterment Association. For a year or so we had been having conversations with Don Glynn and Jerry Kelsh about transferring ownership to the association with the understanding that they would restore the building to its former glory. In the twelve years of our stewardship our remodeling efforts had never gotten above the first floor. The second and third floors and the roof were steadily deteriorating. As evidence of the conditions on the second floor, I submit this conversation overheard early one cold morning.

Jerry: "Boy, the wind is really blowing this morning."

Van: "Have you been outside already?"

Jerry: "No. I'm talking about in my bedroom!"

A new roof was an immediate requirement, as leaks were collapsing the ceiling in the second-floor bedrooms. Van kept searching for some government subsidy that would pay for the repairs and allow us to remain owners, but I finally convinced him that this was wishful thinking. With the Fullerton Centennial only six years away, the good citizens would require at least that much time to raise the necessary funds and complete the restoration. The only caveat to the deal was a verbal agreement that we would have reservation priority for the weekends we wanted to hunt. In the twenty-nine years since, our friends in Fullerton have honored that agreement, once even bumping the governor of North Dakota, whose staff had the temerity to ask for a reservation for the opening of the pheasant season.

As with most projects involving improving the quality of life, the ladies led the way and the guys gradually joined the march. The Carroll House restoration was a community-wide project with more volunteers than a much larger community could produce. The results were fantastic. A complete new cedar-shingle exterior, a bathroom on the second floor, new windows, and central heating, and each bedroom was furnished in late-nineteenth-century décor. All was accomplished in time for the Fullerton Centennial in July of 1987, as was a marvelous history book detailing the first one hundred years of Fullerton. Appropriately, the resplendently restored Carroll House was named to the National Registry of Historical Places in 1994. A tribute to the community-minded citizens of Fullerton.

Three generations of our family now enjoy the Carroll House for one or two weekends every October, and the accommodations are luxurious as compared to forty years ago. So much so that the dogs now have to sleep outside.

FOUR

THE MALLARD KILLER & MORE

My first guest at the Carroll House was Tom Reed. A few years earlier Tom and I had been neighbors in Edina, Minnesota, and my oldest boy, Billy, age eleven, and Tom's son, Tommy, were fast friends. So in September of 1969 the four of us traveled to North Dakota for the early teal season. Because blue-winged and green-winged teal migrated south before the other waterfowl, the federal wildlife people permitted you to hunt them in mid-September, at least three weeks before the regular duck season opened. Without this dispensation, only hunters residing south of Nebraska would get a shot at the speedy teal.

Tom was well acquainted with North Dakota, having come into the world at Carrington, just north of Jamestown, and attended high school in Fargo, graduating in 1940. He was successful in high school as he was in later life, a member of the National Honor Society and an Eagle Scout, and he played all sports in their seasons. He migrated to the University of Minnesota for his further education and graduated in mechanical engineering in 1944, at which time, in accordance with the requirements of the time, the Navy beckoned. Tom was discharged in September of 1946 and went to work for a large manufacturing firm in Minneapolis for $200 per month. The quintessential returning veteran.

When I met Tom in 1960 he was running his company's major division, the residential division, and was a man in full: reliable, resolute, competitive, and with a strong sense of self-worth. He had a tendency toward brusqueness, but I enjoyed every minute we spent together, particularly his competitive nature. He passed away ten years ago this summer, and I still miss him.

Tom loved the Carroll House, but he didn't think

much of the oil burner in the front room, which had been Rob Johnson's living quarters, complete with a hot plate for cooking. The oil burner sputtered and muttered, which Tom couldn't tolerate, so he set to work to repair it. He disassembled the entire device, cleaned everything, and soon had it functioning perfectly. I was so pleased to have invited him, although while the sputtering did bother me, I sort of missed the muttering as I was falling asleep. It sounded like a pleasant, semi-audible conversation between two relaxed hunters. We did shoot some teal that weekend, and Billy shot his first duck, a hen mallard, causing Tom to grumble, "Just like his old man. The first bird he shoots is an illegal one." Which it was. That was a year you could only shoot drakes (males), and besides that the mallard season hadn't opened yet. Tommy didn't have much success shooting, the major problem being he closed both his eyes when he shot, much like Jim Grierson used to do when firing at doves in Mexico. Another story.

The next year the four of us returned to Dickey County to hunt geese. In our wanderings we came across some abandoned goose pits close to the James River, just north of Ludden. There didn't appear to be any other hunters in the neighborhood so we commandeered the pits. They had evidently been dug by a backhoe as they were rectangular, with straight sides, and located about fifty feet apart. It was an ideal situation for us, with Tom and Tommy in one pit and Billy and I in the other.

There weren't many geese flying that chilly, overcast morning and none along the river, so it didn't take much time for ennui to overcome us. An hour or so into our wait, in an attempt to lift our spirits, Tom held up a tin box of cookies and called out, "Would you guys like some cookies?" Having enjoyed only a bowl of cold cereal for breakfast that morning, my son and I responded, "We sure would!"

You don't get much exercise standing in a hole in the ground, so Tom felt the need to stretch his legs. He hoisted himself out of the pit, tucked the cookie container as though it were a football under his arm, and headed for us at a dead run. He ran in a zig-zag manner, dodging tumbleweeds as though they were imaginary tacklers, and switching the cookies from one arm to another à la Walter Payton. Billy and I were impressed.

Then, as he neared our pit, Tom vanished! It was as though he had been wiped off the face of the Earth! The cookie can hit the ground, discharging its contents; his hat slowly floated down, but the Fargo halfback was gone. In actual fact he had fallen in mid-stride into a third goose pit that was filled with dry tumbleweeds, hiding it from our vision. Billy and I jumped out of our pit and ran toward the scene—Billy to rescue the cookies and me to look after Tom. He wasn't hurt, just embarrassed, but pleased to have provided some excitement on an otherwise lackluster morning. A true friend.

Jerry Carlson, a friend and a client of mine, was our second non-family guest. Jerry was a CPA, raised in western Minnesota in the Red River Valley and educated at the University of North Dakota in Grand Forks. For all practical purposes a North Dakotan, so I knew he could easily adapt to the fast-paced lifestyle of Fullerton. I was correct. He enjoyed it so much he brought his ten-year-old son, Kenny, the next year, 1976, and the two of them have been back every year since. They are undemanding guests, never complaining in the early days about the dust or lack of window panes on the second floor and always supplying sweet rolls for breakfast. In addition they are inveterate scouts and were always bringing back information on the whereabouts of water, birds, or new "No Hunting" signs, of which there are more each year.

The first few years after passing his firearms exam at age thirteen, Kenny missed every bird he attempted to shoot. Then one day—perhaps he was seventeen at the time—something clicked and he became able to coordinate the swinging of the shotgun with his vision and thereby acquired the nickname of *The Mallard Killer*, which follows him to this day. He now manages a large credit union in Wisconsin, and I certainly hope his depositors and creditors are not aware of his North Dakota reputation and sobriquet. His two sons, Adam and Grant, are now accompanying their father and grandfather to the Carroll House, so the number of Carlsons in residence on opening weekend has doubled from years ago. Speaking of Grandpa Jerry, he has now taken over Kenny's old position as Chief Bird Misser. Jerry can still shoot, but most of his shots are in the way of a farewell salute as the bird is out of range before he gets the gun up to his shoulder. An affliction that affects many of us older hunters.

Because of Kenny's most pleasant and courteous demeanor he serves as our primary representative to a retired farmer in Ellendale who owns our favorite half-section of CRP. Kenny stays in touch with holiday cards, including family pictures, and subscribes to the Dickey County Leader to keep informed about the news in and around Ellendale. A key part of his mission is to make certain the owner posts "No Hunting" signs on the land prior to the opening of the pheasant season. He has also been called upon to function as the Guide when I feel the need for a break.

Bobby James Cline, who bears a Texas name where the first and middle names are pronounced as one, e.g. Bobbyjames or Billybob, is one of my favorites, as they say on my cell phone. As such he really deserves more mention than a harmless joke at his expense, so here's a quick character study from an unbiased observer.

He was born in 1932 in Floydada, Texas, the county seat of Floyd County, just north of Lubbock in the *Llano Estacado* or staked plains region of west Texas. The area around Floydada is flat and dusty and certainly would qualify for Indian reservation status if they hadn't drilled into the Edwards Aquifer in 1916 and invented irrigation. The most important event prior to that time had been the crossing of that area by Francisco Vásquez de Coronado in 1540 in his search for the golden cities of El Dorado, a trek memorialized by the Conquistador exhibit in the Floydada Historical Society Museum. Because of his distinct facial profile I have long insisted that Bobby is a direct descendent of the Conquistadors. Not from the nobility, you understand, but perhaps from a spear carrier or a cook's helper.

Bobby led a comfortable, middle-class existence in his youth. His father owned a farm implement store as well as some cotton land to the north of town. I have visited Floydada and can assure you there is no Bobby James Cline memorial statue anywhere in the city, so he apparently didn't turn any heads or add to the civic milieu during his developing years. He enrolled at the University of Texas in the fall of 1949 and slumbered through four uneventful and mediocre years at that fine, football factory, which is best known for recruiting running backs shortly after they enter junior high school. He bears a strong allegiance to his alma mater that is best exhibited by the Longhorn emblem on his golf bag, pajamas, and underwear.

Following a two-year stint in the U.S. Navy after college and marriage to sweet Martha Nolen from Waxahachie, Texas, Bobby entered the insurance game. He and I became friends after our two firms, his in Dallas and mine in Minneapolis, were acquired by a national firm on the same day, October 1, 1970, apropos of the merger mania of that time. Within a short time we were exchanging ideas on how to preserve the profitability of our two offices while at the same time circumventing the asinine directives from Corporate. As this process became more time-consuming we felt the need for more extensive communication and started meeting at out-of-the-way venues such as the Carroll House in October.

Bobby was an outdoors guy with hunting, fishing, and golf as his specialties. In all the years I've known him he has only once declined my invitation to engage in any of those three activities. Normally, I had only to give him the date and compass heading and he acquiesced before he knew the activity. I guess he always assumed it was hunting, fishing, or golfing, so why bother with the details. "Just tell me when and where." The one time he declined was last year with some flimsy excuse about his cardiologist having scheduled a procedure to stop his heart and then see if it would start again. I suggested a second opinion, but Bobby had great confidence in the guy because he carried a golf handicap of nine. It struck me as an unrelated credential for choosing your heart doctor.

William F. (Billy) Fellinger is the most avid hunter I know. We became friends about thirty years ago when we lived as neighbors on Lake Minnetonka, and he has been a regular at the Carroll House in October ever since. While the rest of us seldom hunt in any month other than October, Billy has managed to arrange his life so as to engage in the pastime four and sometimes five months a year. And not just on weekends, but for weeks at a time. He easily managed that heavy of a hunting schedule even before he retired some ten years ago, aided by his position on the seniority list of Northwest Airlines pilots and the understanding and gentle ministrations of the Air Line Pilots Association. We all noticed that while retirement was a significant and somewhat scary rite of passage for most of us, for Billy it produced a barely perceptible modification in his lifestyle.

While his wife was well aware before their marriage of Billy's proclivity for wandering off for weeks at a time, she must have assumed he would adjust to a more sedentary pace as he grew older. Such has not been the case, and we all marvel at his outdoor schedule and wonder how he ever had time for his flying duties. A typical year looks something like this:

SEPTEMBER

1-5: Flin Flon, Manitoba–Ducks

13-20: North Dakota–Hungarian Partridge and Sharp-tailed Grouse

OCTOBER

1-7: Flin Flon, Manitoba–Ducks

10-18: North Dakota–Pheasants and Ducks
20-27: Colorado–Ducks

NOVEMBER

6-10: Wisconsin–Deer
16-20: Minnesota–Deer
21-25: North Dakota–Pheasants
26-30: South Dakota–Pheasants

DECEMBER

14-21: North Dakota–Pheasants

JANUARY

11-22: Arizona–Quail

As you can see, he is a consummate outdoorsman, although some of his hunting activities border on obsessive-compulsive behavior. He also harbors another trait that I view as completely addictive. The pothole country of North Dakota is obviously dotted with potholes, and by far the vast majority of them are surrounded by cattails. This is a tall marsh plant of the genus *Phleum* with long, flat, reed-like leaves and long, brown, fuzzy, cylindrical flower spikes. It grows in profusion at the edge of and into the water and is in many instances impossible to traverse. It's even difficult for a dog to walk through cattails. I can't tell you how many times I've entered the cattails, been unable to walk though them, and have had to beat a retreat.

Billy Fellinger, on the other hand, is *addicted* to cattails. I don't know if it is the pungent marsh smell or the fluffy seeds in his eyes, ears, and mouth that attracts him, or whether it's because that's where the smart, old roosters hide. At any rate, when cresting a small rise and glimpsing a pothole to his right or left, he will deviate from course, bear down into the cattails, dogs in tow, and disappear from sight. As he slithers deep into the heart of the cattails his presence there is only noticeable when a startled rooster erupts from the thicket. As the cattails average seven or eight feet in height, none of us can understand how he manages to see the birds, let alone shoot them. He must be shooting at the sound they make as they thrash about in an attempt to get airborne à la Joe Shuster. Billy, by the way, is an excellent shot, certainly the best in our group, and misses very few birds in flight. He could easily be a professional hunter.

However, he is most famous in Fullerton for driving his truck smack into a telephone pole located in the middle of the street between the Carroll House and the grain elevator. Literally tens of thousands of trucks, over the years, loaded with grain, have passed that pole on their way to and from the elevator and never come close to it, but Billy managed to hit it square on. A feat even more amazing in that the pole was located only thirty-five feet from his departure point. He was just leaving to return home and evidently became distracted when he dropped a ball-point pen and reached down to retrieve it. Most of our group was outside waving him goodbye and were astonished to see an airplane driver unable to steer a truck around a telephone pole.

When I next saw him again, in Minneapolis, I questioned his motor skills and coordination by asking, "Billy, how do you manage to raise the flaps or lower the landing gear on a 747?"

He nonchalantly replied, "Oh, the co-pilot does that."

When we returned the following October we saw that the boys from the elevator had encircled the infamous pole with three mobile fertilizer tanks to protect it from Captain Billy. We obviously weren't the only ones to witness his accident.

I met another of my favorites, Joe Chenoweth, on a goose hunting trip to Chihuahua, Mexico, sponsored by Tom Reed in 1983. I was invited on the trip as Tom's friend and Joe as his protégé. By protégé I mean only that Joe was following in Tom's footsteps as head of the Residential Division, then as head of the International Company in Brussels and eventually back to Minneapolis as one of several prospective CEOs in waiting, a position not at all to his liking, resulting in early retirement. When I met Joe, he was just forty-seven years of age, an engineering graduate of Montana State, and had been with Tom's firm for twenty-three years. A capable executive, whose overriding characteristics were sincerity and a calm, assertive energy. Joe was unflappable; just what you would expect from a good Norwegian.

Over the years Joe had developed a technique for dealing with the management stresses of corporate life. While others around him were losing their cool and calling down incantations on the competition and the unions, Joe was gradually sinking into a Zen-like state. It got to the point that his subordinates were afraid to mention another problem to be confronted for fear he would lose consciousness altogether. This capacity to relax under duress was an admirable trait, but the stress of accomplishing that feat caused his hair to turn grey at age thirty-five. This made him look wiser and even more serene, which only added to his "no drama" reputation.

When Joe bought a ranch near Roscoe, Montana, prior to his retirement he was still traveling the world for the International Company. He would fly into Billings and drive down to his property a few times a year, causing his neighbors to speculate as to what his occupation was. No one they knew dropped by on their return from Tokyo or Riyadh. Gradually, the consensus developed that he was employed by the CIA, which they viewed as only a slight improvement over the KGB. It has taken him several years to overcome this misconception, but he will probably never convince all of the locals that the company he worked for was not *the* Company.

Born and raised in Montana, Joe much prefers

big-game hunting from his Jeep to walking over the prairie in search of upland game. It's also a tough six-hundred-mile drive from his ranch to the Carroll House. The last time he made that trek it rained the entire trip which, as any of you who have driven ten or twelve hours in a pouring rain know, is extremely tiring. When Joe arrived in early evening at the Carroll House he was barely able to climb out of his truck. Two whiskeys later he was starting to recover, but by the time we walked down to the Ranch House and sat down for dinner, a semi-comatose state had enveloped him. So much so that when the waitress brought Joe his steak he roused himself gamely and announced, "No thanks. I've already eaten." My son, Scott, recognizing Joe's delicate condition, encouraged him to eat his dinner by saying, "That's okay Joe. Have another," to which Joe, in a stoic state of agree-ability replied, "Okay," and enthusiastically consumed his steak. All of us at the table could only wonder, there but for the grace of God go I. A solid eight hours of sleep did wonders for him and eliminated all memory of his lengthy journey the previous day.

Last but not least of my outdoor associates are my two sons, Bill and Scott. I certainly can't speak for them, but the time we have spent together hunting in North Dakota, fishing in Canada, and golfing together wherever have created my most cherished memories. Forty years ago, when Bill was eleven and Scott was nine, I remember them climbing the box elder tree next to the Carroll House and shooting at sparrows out of the second floor windows with their BB guns. That tree is now gone and the windows are no longer without glass, but the memory is still very real.

In the early years we would drive to Fullerton for at least two weekends every October. When the Minnesota teachers held their annual convention in mid-October and the boys were out of school, we would leave on Thursday afternoon, otherwise we were on the road right after school on Friday. They always enjoyed the drive, the changing scenery, and the stop at the drive-in in Glenwood, Minnesota. We would stop at the granite marker by Lake Minnewaska, eat our hamburgers, and read from the bronze plaque about the glaciers that had formed the surrounding countryside. Simple pleasures. On the ride home the boys and Mandy slept in the back of the station wagon with the backseat flattened, and I struggled to keep my eyes open. We were always very tired but happy when we arrived at home.

In the 1970s both boys were enjoying their adolescence, and it was an ideal time for them to spend time with adult males who were good role models. Most of my friends at that time were just hitting their stride in terms of business success, solid family relationships, and concern and respect for their fellow man. Their spirits were high, and they thrived on good-hearted banter, which they took as well as they delivered. The boys laughed so hard at some of their antics and comments they fell off my mother's old couch.

High-school athletics interfered with some October weekends for Bill, but Scott continued to be a regular until he was bitten by the acting bug and moved to California. Bill returned for the annual get-together after his college years, and Scott would come from California when his work allowed. By this time they were both surpassing me in terms of stamina and shooting skills. It was a pleasure for the three of us to work together in a small slough, using hand signals and experience to flush the birds. As the pheasant habitat improved and the birds returned in numbers we had gradually moved away from hunting ducks and geese to spending more time hunting pheasants. Not only do pheasants taste better, but they are much easier to clean and don't require the tedious placement of decoys.

Starting about ten years ago, two of the grandsons, Thane and Will, reached the required age to accompany us to the Carroll House. Scott's boy, Thane, is more enthusiastic about all aspects of hunting, including cleaning the birds, than his cousin Will. Now that I think about it, his dad, my own son Bill, always seemed to disappear at bird-cleaning time as well. I overhear from time to time some of the advice and direction I used to give my boys being reconstituted and passed on to the youngsters from their dads. That will bring a smile to your face.

I am also indebted to my sons for convincing me to undergo knee-replacement surgery some fifteen years ago. We were walking, some seven or eight of us in a line, through a half-section of CRP land, and my boys—and I must admit, several others—were being critical of my pace. By critical, I mean they were saying things like, "Go back to the truck, Dad, you're too slow." And then from Bobby Cline, "If you walk much farther, you won't be able to go back and we're not going to carry you!" I was both hurt and angry. These guys wouldn't even know how to locate this field if it weren't for me. And two of them wouldn't even be on this planet if it weren't for me. That did it, I had knee surgery two months later, and have been walking fine ever since. Oh, I do need some assistance if I step in a badger hole, but no one seems to be bothered by that.

FIVE

THE INTERNATIONAL MEETING

In 1976, Jacques d'Arfeuille was in Minneapolis for a week, attending meetings with his boss at their corporate headquarters. His boss, Allen Brosius, was the risk manager for the parent company, and Jacques held the same position for their French subsidiary. As their insurance broker, I worked closely with both of them and was asked to sit in on some of their tête-á-têtes as a combination facilitator and translator, as Allen had a tin ear insofar as Jacques's English was concerned. It was actually more of a cultural than a language problem. Jacques had a tendency to answer most of Al's requests with a, "That is impossible!" with the accent on the third syllable, when in the true French way what he meant was "That would be difficult." Not impossible, but difficult. By "difficult" he usually meant he didn't want to explain Al's request to his superiors in Paris and thereby lose his independence. This is very typical of a corporate parent/subsidiary relationship. So my job was to persuade Jacques to at least give it a try.

On Thursday of that week I asked Jacques if he was returning to Paris on the weekend.

"No," he answered, "I am going to Montreal to visit a cousin and then back to Paris on Monday." "Jacques," I countered, "Why would you want to go to Montreal, where everyone speaks French, when you could accompany me to North Dakota for the weekend and realize an entirely new experience? We will stay at the Chateau Carroll, hunt canards, and observe the local citizenry, which I assure you will broaden your horizons. This is an opportunity to walk through the sloughs of a country you've never seen before." Oh, what a salesman I was in those days! Jacques didn't hesitate. He cancelled his reservations for Montreal, and we set out for Fullerton at noon of the next day.

Like most Europeans on their first land voyage

across “flyover country,” Jacques was enthralled with the rich farmland and open spaces. When we reached the North Dakota border, he pondered on the distance travelled and commented, “We would be in Austria by now.” The prairie can be a bit intimidating to many newcomers, particularly Europeans. The horizons are so far and the land so vast and sparsely settled that, unless you were raised on the steppes of Russia, it’s somewhat unnerving. While Jacques was a Parisian, he did visit his country house in central France on weekends, so he was somewhat familiar with rural life.

I knew Joe Shuster was coming up for the weekend and bringing a friend. To our amazement his friend, one Roland Conte, was also from Paris. So my plan to immerse Jacques in the English language and American culture was somewhat diluted. However, Roland was a delight, an unusual blend of physicist and economist who spoke English in profane bursts. By that I mean that his English consisted only of swear words and oaths learned as a youngster from the American GIs who had liberated France. He could rattle them off in rapid fashion and managed to communicate without once ever having to resort to a normal vocabulary. Of course, the French accent overlaid all the syllables so that sometimes it seemed his statements were direct from Chaucer and at other times he appeared to be speaking Welsh. I regret to this day not having had a tape recorder at hand.

Those were the days when we prepared our meals at the Carroll House. The menu was always the same: lasagna on Friday night, which we heated in my mother's old gas stove, which I had rescued from the Salvation Army, and steaks prepared on the charcoal grill on Saturday night. When Tom Reed was in residence we were treated to the most marvelous Margauxs and Pomerals to enhance the meal. An integral part of the Friday meal was lighting the gas oven. As our fuel was propane, a heavy gas that tends to settle rather than drift up into the atmosphere, striking a match near the oven door always produced a small explosion resulting from time to time in the instantaneous removal of eyebrows. No one who had performed the act ever volunteered for an encore, so every Friday evening in camp I had to carefully select an unsuspecting neophyte to perform this vital service. Over time this selection process assumed the characteristics of a ritual initiation ceremony.

As the time grew near to light the oven, the experienced guests would drift towards the kitchen from the living room and congregate in the doorway. As I lifted the lasagna from the Coleman cooler, my gaze would settle on the victim and casually, almost distractedly, I would ask, "Joe, would you light the oven, please? The matches are there on the shelf." On this October evening in 1976 I couldn't really ask Joe Shuster, as his recollection of last year's lighting was still vivid in his mind. In the interest of

Franco-American relations I obviously couldn't designate Jacques or Roland. So it boiled down to a choice between my old college roommate, Dick Murphy, or my old handball partner, Charley Schuler. It was an agonizing choice, but time was fleeting and the group assembled in the doorway was growing impatient. So... "Charley, would you light the oven, please? The matches are there on the shelf."

The muffled explosion that resulted brought cheers and laughter from the boys in the doorway and a startled look from Charley, but no eyebrow loss—just a reddening of the cheeks that would pass quickly.

Hunting that weekend was not particularly good. There were few pheasants, the geese weren't down from Canada yet, and the duck hatch was patchy that year, but we had a wonderful time. The two Frenchmen were interested in everything and asked questions of the nearest American at hand. Roland turned out to be an accomplished salad chef, while Jacques helped wash dishes and served coffee in the morning. Odd little things, such as canned corn, which evidently wasn't available in Paris, intrigued him. I seem to recall he even took a can back to Paris to show his wife.

While the hunting around Fullerton was mediocre, the social event of the year took place that weekend. The bar had changed ownership, resulting in a gala staged by the new owner, Wayne Ulmer, on Saturday night. A gala, to Wayne's way of thinking, involved free beer and brats, guaranteeing an overflow crowd. It would be very different not having Bee (Bernard) Simek presiding behind the bar, so we were all curious to meet the new owner and gauge his personality.

As we all know, the proprietor of a bar or tavern serves many roles: friend, advisor, sometimes confessor, and always a dispenser of good cheer. Bee's place, over the years, had naturally taken on his personality, which focused on a laissez-faire attitude with few behavior boundaries. This attitude was coupled with a sense of continuity and resistance to change. They like to tell the story about Bee leaning over the bar and solemnly addressing several of his regular patrons:

"Boys, I'm very sorry about this, but I have to raise the price of drinks to thirty-five cents from thirty cents." Seeing their disappointment he offered, "But, I'll sell you three for a dollar."

I always enjoyed walking into the place after a year's absence, declaring "drinks for the house," and covering the tab with a $5 bill. The thing that also appealed to me about the joint was that kids and dogs were always welcome. Well, Bee's Bar was no longer. Wayne had renamed it the Ranch House and eventually would enlarge the place, install a kitchen, and serve meals, which was absolutely necessary as Ruby had closed her café. Dogs are no longer permitted, which is unfortunate, as their manners were considerably better than some of the human clientele, and they so enjoyed being part of the festivities.

A large crowd assembled at the Ranch House that fine October evening. Most of the farmers in the area and their families were there when we walked in after dinner. As the party progressed and the crowd became more talkative, I caught glimpses of Jacques and Roland in the melée from time to time. They were both engaged in animated conversations with various farmers. Jacques was more than dressed for the occasion, sporting a blue blazer and a cerise cravet around his neck, matching his complexion as the evening wore on. The Ranch House became a North Dakota version of the Tower of Babel. The presence of the two Europeans seemed to bring out the latent native languages of the patrons, and I heard snippets of Bohemian, Norwegian, German, and of course, French.

My responsibilities as host, guide, and chief cook regrettably always required me to be the first to leave the bar, to be prepared for the morrow. I had to be content to vicariously enjoy the events of the night before at the retelling over the next morning's coffee. Early reports that Sunday morning indicated a potentially major catastrophe had occurred after my departure the night before. One of the farmer friends of Jacques, in a gesture of conviviality, had given him a chew of tobacco. (I learned many years later the supplier was the estimable Duke of Dickey, Don Glynn.) Poor Jacques, without any experience with

Wintergreen Skoal, had chewed the substance, liked the taste and then swallowed it. His digestive system, while impervious to whiskey and red wine followed by beer, couldn't tolerate the additional narcotic and rebelled. He had become very ill. Jerry Carlson reported that on one of his nocturnal trips to sniff the air he had encountered Jacques, dressed only in his underwear, sitting on the side porch with his head in his hands at 3:45 in the morning. The temperature at the time was twenty-eight degrees.

My son, Scott, came into the kitchen to announce that "Mr. d'Arfeuille says he won't be down for breakfast."

We always had a morning hunt on Sunday before returning to Minnesota, and missing that was not an issue. What could be a problem, however, was Jacques missing the flight from Aberdeen to Minneapolis, which in turn would cause him to miss his connection to New York and then to Paris that same day. I needn't have worried. When I returned from dispersing the boys at Herman's Slough at 9:00 A.M. there stood Monsieur d'Arfeuille in the side yard of the Carroll House. He was resplendent in the early morning light, dressed in last night's finery, with his suitcase at his feet.

On closer examination however, it was obvious that Jacques was a shell of the bon vivant of yesterday. His eyes in particular were disturbing in that they were completely lifeless, yet from their depths the most agonizing pain was obvious. The memory of those eyes still haunts me. In my judgment this guy would not survive the trip to Paris. He might not even survive the trip to Aberdeen. My hunting vehicle at the time was a 1976 International Harvester Scout equipped with the shortest possible wheelbase, which made proceeding in a straight line almost impossible. At fifty-five miles per hour the Jeep-like contraption would hop from side to side, not dangerously, but enough to make you keep your feet braced. In Jacques's condition he felt it necessary to brace both his feet and hands.

For some reason having to do with the rag-top, dust from the gravel roads was sucked into the interior as though by a giant vacuum, adding to the discomfort of the ride. The one-hour trip to Aberdeen was conducted in absolute silence. Jacques sat rigid and stared straight ahead, his face covered with a thin film of dust, adding to his pallor. At the airport we bid *adieu,* no more, and he boarded the plane. I gave him no chance of reaching Paris alive. His last breath would probably take place somewhere over the North Atlantic.

Imagine my surprise and relief when I received the following letter (*next page*) from Jacques a few days later.

As you can see, there was no mention of his near-death experience or the suffering he had endured on that Sunday morning. The ability of the human mind to suppress such trauma is indeed a marvel and is most highly developed in gala attendees.

J. D'ARFEUILLE

Tél. : 43.66

Date 10/13/76

~~A l'attention de M~~

Dear Bill

I enjoyed this week end at Fullerton and I thank you very much for your hearty welcome. It was very interesting for me to know North Dakota and I appreciated very much to live during two days with you and your friends who were so friendly and kind with me. (If you have a moment, please let me know their name, because my listing is incomplete).

I confirm you, Bill, that we would be very glad of welcoming Scott next summer. We think that the best time for his visit here would be from July 10th till ~~[illegible]~~ august 3 or 4th, because after Olivier will take a job. Our vacation plans are not yet decided upon, but I think we'll leave Paris on July 13d for our country house where we'll stay during four weeks.

Yours sincerely

Jacques

SIX

STANDING ROCK

In 1970, Van married a Catholic widow gal from Owatonna who also had six children. To please her he adopted ballroom dancing as a new hobby. I always felt the dancing was a healthy activity that also provided them with an escape from his and her "Gang of Twelve." In an effort to bond with the two youngest of his new step-children, Danny and Mike Viehman, he decided to take them on a hunting trip in early September, before school started. As a backup for his parental outreach he wanted me and my two boys, who were approximately the same age as the Viehman boys, to accompany them on the trip.

As the geese didn't migrate into Dickey County until mid-October and the pheasant season didn't open until the same time, Van had decided to travel to the west side of the Missouri River to the habitat of the wily sharp-tailed grouse. We had never hunted sharp-tail before, but that only made the invitation more intriguing. Upland birds are upland birds; some are just faster than others.

With six of us going on the trip, we decided to stay in a motel in Fort Yates, North Dakota, an Indian town in the center of the Standing Rock Reservation and the site of Sitting Bull's grave. This reservation extends into South Dakota, and there is another grave site there as well, just south of Mobridge, but the one in Fort Yates is deemed the correct location because it has the largest monument and attracts more visitors. Fort Yates sits on the west bank of the Missouri River some sixty miles south of Mandan. Mandan, of course, is the location of historic Fort Abraham Lincoln, established in 1872, and the jumping-off point for the 7th Calvary on their ill-fated expedition to the Little Bighorn River in Montana in the summer of 1876, led by that paragon of military hubris, Lieutenant Colonel George Armstrong Custer.

Halfway between Mandan and Fort Yates, on the

West River Road, you cross the Cannonball River where it empties into the wide Missouri. Almost miraculously this river over the ages has been able to tumble and bounce large boulders down its course and shape them gradually into perfect spheres, much like cannonballs, only larger in many instances. Of course these round rocks were attractive to the Native Americans, and they collected many but found them too heavy to transport on their nomadic forays to summer and winter camps. When the original white settlers arrived, they too found the rocks attractive, and many a driveway in Morton and Grant Counties are marked by stone cannonballs, usually painted white. I have always yearned for one of these river-worn relics but have never found one just laying alongside the road. They're much too attractive.

If you drive south out of Mandan after dark you become aware of Fort Yates about the time you cross the Cannonball. It's a bright light on the southern horizon about thirty miles away. This illumination is but another achievement of the Bureau of Indian Affairs (BIA) in Washington, D.C. In the winter, or roughly six months of the year, pitch blackness descended over western North Dakota about 4:00 P.M. In the early 1960s the Tribal Council petitioned the BIA for some streetlights to assist them in finding their way home to their little government houses in the dark.

The government responded to this request by awarding

a cost-plus, no-bid contract to an electrical company owned by a cousin of one of the state's senators. This fine gentleman installed a lighting system for Fort Yates that can be recognized from the space shuttle. Thomas Edison in 1883 electrified New York City with streetlights in his pursuit of the glorification of light, but the BIA managed to exceed Edison's work by a factor of ten. The problem for the Hunkpapa Sioux was no longer darkness but rather such extreme illumination as to make it impossible to sleep. The rumor is that the senator's cousin retired early and bought a pineapple plantation in Hawaii.

We secured reservations at the Warrior Motel, one of the few businesses in town and owned by a white couple. A white man also owned the tavern, which opened its door at 10:00 A.M. to an enthusiastic crowd. Having lived for a time as a youngster near the Lower Brule Reservation in South Dakota, I was very familiar with the effects of the government policy that kept the Indians on welfare for generations, without meaningful work, education, or future prospects, resulting in a high level of alcoholism. After a long hot day spent navigating the hills and coulees above the town, I stopped at the tavern in late afternoon to buy a six-pack of cold beer. After taking one step into the place I decided to keep one foot outside the door in the event that a quick exit was necessary. I'm normally not squeamish about dark places, but the dark in there was ominous.

I could hear but not see a couple of ladies having a violent argument in the back and barely made out the shapes of several gents with their heads down on the bar. They had obviously been there from the opening bell. The proprietor, a young man in his mid-thirties, brought me my six-pack. In his other hand he carried a sawed-off baseball bat, which resembled a policeman's night stick on steroids. When I inquired about it he informed me he had several other similar bats placed strategically behind the bar so that one was always within reach. His eyes kept sweeping around the interior, and he was obviously in a state of alertness. He had owned the joint for two years and expected to save enough money through the next year to retire. I wished him good luck and good health and beat a hasty retreat. It reminded me of the bar scene in *Star Wars* but with a less attractive clientele.

We enjoyed the hunt on the Standing Rock Reservation after adjusting to the take-off speed of the grouse. Whereas a pheasant takes some time to reach maximum acceleration, a sharp-tail is much quicker, maybe because they are smaller. They emit a clucking noise when startled and, like all upland birds, enjoy getting airborne from right under your feet. It is similar to pheasant hunting in that you have to walk for hours in order to entice enough birds to flush. It is dissimilar in that grouse tend to explode upwards in groups or coveys, rather than singly, and fly off in different directions. I'm assuming they rendezvous later and giggle over the startled looks on the hunters' faces caused by their lift-off.

We walked up and down the hillsides and coulees just west of the river. There wasn't much agriculture on the reservation, mostly open land, with a few small fields of alfalfa. Walking uphill with your eyes on the ground made me aware of how the vegetation changed about every hundred feet. Obviously there was less moisture being retained in the ground the higher you went, and the plants were different in very distinct bands going up the hill. With no formal training in botany, seeing such adaptation at work made a great impression on me. That's another benefit to hunting. You see some pretty amazing things.

It was a warm weekend in early September, and the dogs tired quickly as did our young hunters, but we did accomplish the purpose of our trip. Van and his step-sons grew to know each other better, and we brought home some grouse. My boys acquired some valuable and enduring lessons about reservation life, and I learned how to pronounce "Sitting Bull" in the Sioux language.

SEVEN

KASKATTOMAGAN

One would think that decades of hunting, chasing, and sometimes shooting migratory waterfowl in the Missouri–Mississippi flyways with *all* types of hunting companions would provide one with some degree of circumspection and cool as far as a hunting trip is concerned. Over the years, I've hunted with experts, novices, guys who wanted to listen to the ballgame, guys who wanted to sleep, claimers, drinkers, and once even a game warden. I've fallen out of boats, stepped in over my waders, been stuck in the loon-stuff more times than I care to remember, carried decoys and sometimes birds for miles, and in general had a ball trying to save the people in Texas, Louisiana, and Rochester from being inundated by our feathered friends. I've blown easy shots along the Missouri in South Dakota, over the potholes in Saskatchewan, beside the Delta in Manitoba, and in the sloughs of North Dakota since I was a kid. If there were some birds in Minnesota I'd enjoy missing them, too.

None of this experience and background, however, prepared me in the slightest for the trip I took to Hudson Bay in September of 1968 in search of the *Branta canadensis.* Aside from the fact that we hunted a thousand miles north of Minneapolis, what made this trip unique were my hunting companions. Going to Hudson Bay in itself was enough romance for me, but journeying with the likes of *Bob Bartholemay, Dave Burkholder, Dick Garmaker, D'Arcy Leck, John Sagehorn,* and *Joe Shuster* made me positively aquiver. Just run through that roster again and see if *you* don't quiver.

The Plan, as outlined by the Great White Guide Garmaker, was to meet in Winnipeg, Manitoba, on Saturday night so as to be ready to leave for the 58th parallel at 7:30 on Sunday morning. An advance party of Bart, Leck, and the guide arrived a day early to check out the weather and find the best deal on supplies. In so doing they blew out a tire and D'Arcy's digestive system, and the G.W. Guide got lost. The rest of us arrived at the appointed time to find that part of the supplies had been already consumed, but Bart had excellent meteorological information concerning western Alberta. No one had the foggiest idea what the weather was on the southwest shore of Hudson Bay, but Bart knew it was snowing in Alberta and the front was moving east. Northwest pilots seem to be preoccupied with fronts. I supposed it's their environment.

We spent all day Sunday in the motel receiving various departure times from Tom Ruminsky, the owner of God's River Lodge and the goose camp, interspersed with weather prognostications from Bart and directional orders from John, who had appointed himself head of the search party for the G.W.G., who was lost again. Learning finally that the weather at God's Lake was bad and that we wouldn't leave until Monday, we retired to Joe's room to watch the Vikings demolish Green Bay and Anthony Quinn dance through *Zorba the Greek.*

Thus refreshed, we left Winnipeg the next morning in a Twin Otter thoughtfully provided by Midwest Airlines and Ruminsky. I had anticipated a Cessna 180 with floats, and the sight of those two turboprops did much to restore my faith in the guide as well as the possibility of arriving at our destination, the Kaskattomagan River. The Otter is the workhorse of the Canadian bush country as roads are nonexistent. Everything moves by air. This particular aircraft had space for the seven of us, all our gear, and the camp supplies, with room left over for a large stack of four-by-eight-foot sheets of plywood in the midsection. We unloaded the plywood and some of the supplies at a refueling spot at God's Lake, which is roughly halfway between Winnipeg and the goose camp.

Leaving God's Lake after refueling, we proceeded on our northeasterly course into a sudden fog. There will be some members of the group who will tell you we flew under the fog and skimmed the treetops into Kaska. There are even some who doubted the wisdom of the trip at this point, but I assure you that the altimeter *never* registered below three hundred feet. It's the first time I've ever flown and spotted geese *above* me, however.

Landing at the strip at the camp in the fog was a thrill, considering that other than three oil barrels sitting on the muskeg, there were no other identifying markers to indicate where to land. We immediately broke out the shotguns and darted off into the fog, so happy to be on terra firma. I have wasted many hours attempting to crawl up on feeding geese and long ago learned the futility of that method, but D'Arcy did it! That tells you how bad the fog was. Returning to camp, which consisted of a shack and attached lean-to, we spent a pleasant evening recounting the picturesque flight in and wondering if the fog would ever lift. Dave and I elected to sleep in the lean-to as a compromise between trying to sleep in the same room with the Great White Guide and the tent occupied by our three Cree guides. On reflection, it would have been a lot warmer in the tent, but then we would have missed all that wonderful singing.

The next day, Tuesday, was a hunter's dream. We arose at 4:00 A.M., followed the Indians to the shore of the ocean in the dark, and managed to run out of shells by 9:30. We did have thirty-five geese, however, which isn't too bad considering that only thirty-five thousand flew over our heads. Mostly Canadian honkers, with a few blues and snows. After a quick lunch we hurried down the river about a mile to a spot Ruminsky recommended for brook trout. As Burkholder qualified as the only piscatorialist in the group, one of the guides waded him another mile or so down the river where the big ones lay. At our location, Sagehorn had the first strike and managed to lose about a four-pound brookie, but it wasn't long before the G.W. Guide, Joe, and Bart were pulling them in with regularity. D'Arcy and I rested our eyes in preparation for the evening shoot and, in a couple hours, the fishermen had a string of twenty or twenty-five trout. Dave then returned from his expedition loaded down with a lone little fish, much to everyone's delight, and we adjourned to the hunting grounds. Ho hum, another dozen honkers added during the evening shoot. Not a bad day.

Now that the fog had lifted, we could survey our surroundings and get some idea as to the ecosystem at the northern boundary of the boreal forest and the beginning of the tundra. The only trees in this neighborhood were stunted and restricted to the river banks. The Kaskattomagan River is one of several rivers in northern Manitoba draining into Hudson Bay from the southwest. As it nears the ocean, the Kaska divides into six channels, creating many islands. These islands provide a safe nesting area for tens of thousands of geese, which is of course why we were there. It is a remote area, six hundred miles northeast of Winnipeg and sparsely settled by humans. Our guides were Cree Indians from York Factory, former headquarters for the Hudson Bay Company, one hundred miles to the west.

Wednesday was a similar operation with a few exceptions. We didn't waste quite as many shells in getting our birds, and Dave lived up his credentials, catching twenty-six fish by himself. The wind was stronger, so the geese flew higher, and D'Arcy drove them higher yet with his three-inch Howitzer. His gun jammed during the morning hunt, but he surely produced some profit for good old Federal Cartridge in the P.M. We also learned a little about high tide and flooded creeks and wet feet on this day. Now we understood why the guides were there.

Thursday was supposed to be our last day in camp, so we got an early start for the shore. I lucked out with the best location and had eight honkers in the blind within two hours. Life was good! Then one of the Indians wandered by and inquired politely if I would like to leave and return to camp. I informed him equally politely but firmly that I was having a fine time and didn't intend to leave for at least another couple of hours. Then he asked if I had noticed the *polar bear*? *What* polar bear? (Not quite as politely!) Following his pointing finger across the river I *noticed* the polar bear. It was a yellowish color, not having yet converted to its white winter coat, but it was enormous and only about a hundred yards away, proceeding toward the coast. Quickly calculating the firepower of my twelve-gauge, the length of time required by the bear to cross the shallow river—maybe ten seconds—and that I was already over my limit, I reconsidered my plans and informed the guide politely, "Pick up the geese, and let's get out of here!"

Leisurely sauntering past Joe's blind I was challenged as to why I was abandoning the field so early. Upon learning about my friend across the river, Joe allowed as how he would walk along to keep me company. So endeth the morning shoot!

Several weeks after our return to civilization, Tom Ruminksy called to update us on our polar bear friend. It seems the animal had wandered into camp, noticed the geese hanging on the wall of the lean-to, and proceeded to have lunch. According to Tom, the bear stood up with his left paw on the roof of the building, which was eight feet in height, and proceeded to devour ten geese. The hunters in camp cowered in the shack and prayed he wouldn't require dessert after lunch.

Thursday afternoon was another "wait for the airplane drill" without benefit of the Packers, although the G.W.G. did a fairly good imitation of Zorba. John took time out from stretching my cap to fish some more, and Bart resumed his weather forecasting. The rest of us did what comes naturally on a wet, foggy afternoon on the Kaska: played poker. Our genial host, Ruminsky, laid in a few acorns and a fair supply of antifreeze for the winter at that session.

At sundown, having reconciled himself to the fact that the Otter wasn't going to reach Kaska that day, the Great White Guide, in a self-induced state of megalomania, appointed himself the Commissioner of Indian Affairs in northeastern Manitoba and rationed out a bit of our supplies to our good Cree friends. It was an interesting social and physiological experiment that resulted in ruining a good night's sleep for most of us. Prior to being introduced to strong spirits, my guide, Alex Yellowback, a somber and taciturn young man, had exhibited perfect manners and decorum.

After downing roughly twelve ounces of scotch whiskey in a matter of minutes, he transformed into a wild-eyed evangelist for the Native Cause. With his unkempt long hair down over his bloodshot eyes, and spittle cascading down his chin, he more resembled a wild animal than a Cree brave. His two companions had also experienced the same transformation, and the three of them were huddled in their tent gazing sadly at the empty whiskey bottle when I entered to take their rifle as a precautionary measure. They protested mightily but seemed unable to reach a standing position to prevent the seizure. Finally reaching his feet, Alex Yellowback bolted out into the night, howling like a wolf.

Have you ever spent three hours in the bush, the northern lights flickering merrily above, searching for a Cree brave who mentally has metamorphosed into a wolf? Believe me, it's enough to make you vote for a new commissioner. I did pick up a fair amount of the local colloquialisms that evening and can attest that "white dog" etc. is not necessarily a term of endearment. T'was a night to remember!

Reliable Midwest Airlines arrived on Friday morning, and we loaded our limit of geese and trout into the plane with a sincere feeling of regret. We had been to Hudson Bay, where the Kaskattomagan divides into six rivers and pours into the most westerly cove of the Atlantic Ocean. A divergent yet compatible group of bedfellows to be known henceforth as the White Dogs of Kaska.

EIGHT

"THE GUIDE SHOOTS FIRST"

Joe Shuster and I missed meeting each other at the University of Minnesota in the early 1950s, which is not surprising in that there were fifty thousand students on campus and we were in different fields of study, Joe in the School of Engineering, complete with slide rule, and I in pre-med originally and later science, literature and the arts (S.L.A.). We were introduced some ten years after graduation by a mutual friend, Dick Garmaker. Over the succeeding forty-odd years we have shared much time and many thoughts together, although you have to be on your toes, figuratively speaking, to carry on a conversation with Joe. His mind is extremely agile, and he is the best I've ever known at nuance and braiding disparate but related points into a common theme. Maybe the best way to describe his mental agility is that his spontaneous response to an issue, large or small, is the one you would have provided after a night to think about it. I'm usually a step behind Joe, which might, in part, be attributed to my attempting to always stay on my toes.

In 1962, Joe founded a cryogenics company in New Prague, Minnesota, called Minnesota Valley Engineering and built it into one of the largest cryogenic equipment manufacturers in the world. His passion for science and attention to detail, coupled with innate leadership characteristics, contributed to his executive skills. He also had the advantage of spending his formative years in one of the most notorious environments in America, living in the Cabrini-Green Public Housing Project on the near north side of Chicago, which provided him with an unvarnished view of human nature. Joe can spot a phony from across the street and around the corner and has antennae that are attuned to plausible but not genuine reasoning. He does, however, have some difficulty, as many of us do, in recognizing his own specious behavior when it comes to admitting an error in judgment. We shall address this failing in a moment.

In the fall of 1978 a number of my friends and I had gathered at the Carroll House for a weekend of hunting and conviviality. Included in the gathering were Joe Shuster, Dick Garmaker and his two boys, Steve and Stuart, Dick Mast, the Carlsons, Jerry and Ken the Mallard Killer, Scott Baker, and myself. It was mid-October, and the geese were down from Canada and the duck population was on the rise, so waterfowl hunting was excellent. Some meticulous scouting on the part of the Carlsons had secured the intelligence that Herman Zimbelman's slough at dusk was crowded with maybe a thousand mallards and five hundred snow geese that had selected our favorite slough as their overnight rest area. That many birds in a slough of that size was unheard of and most unusual.

While numbers like that are exciting, they actually complicate a guide's life. We would need a careful and seamless strategy in order to surround the slough at least an hour before daylight and hope for a cloudy day in order to thwart fifteen hundred pairs of eyes and ears. I even considered spending the night in position next to the water in order to be ready when the mallards went out to feed before sunup. In North Dakota you can shoot half an hour before sunup which sometimes provides enough light for duck shooting. Geese don't like to get up that early. Their preference is to leave for breakfast sometime between 8:00 and 9:00 A.M., but shooting at the ducks would probably convince them to reluctantly leave the slough.

Past experience had taught me the infeasibility of outlining a plan to the other hunters the evening before the shoot, because at least half of them couldn't retain the data until the following morning. This was particularly true of the guys who weren't familiar with the terrain and were also the guys most enjoying their cocktails during the lecture. On this particular Friday night that description fit exactly half of the assembly. On the other hand this plan was so complicated and so detailed that there might not be time to cover it all in the morning.

So, against my better judgment, I carried the chalkboard to the living room and began the chalk talk. Seven of the boys were assigned to approach the target from the southwest, with five of them spread out in the reeds around that quadrant of the slough and the Carlsons stationed in a rock pile located directly to the south. Meanwhile, Garmaker and I would sneak in from the southeast, carrying the goose decoys. We would place the decoys on a slight rise just to the southeast, trusting the geese would see them when they arose and turn towards the two of us. Everyone was cautioned to move slowly and quietly and be in place by 6:15 A.M., just one hour before sunrise and a half hour before legal shooting time.

The next morning I quickly reviewed the plan and reminded Scott to keep close watch over Mast and Shuster, as neither of them appeared to be completely awake at that early hour—undoubtedly the result of some over-serving at Bee's place the previous night. Gar and I hoisted the goose decoys into the back of my station wagon, the others clambered into two other vehicles, and we set off in the dark for Herman's slough.

HERMAN'S SLOUGH

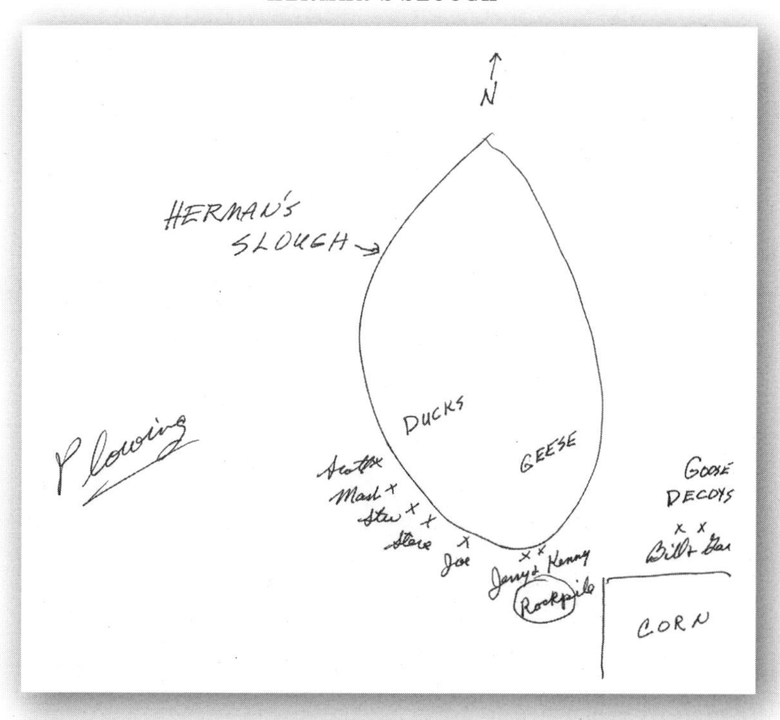

Both groups parked about three-quarters of a mile from their destination. The seven of them from the southwest walked across a plowed field, and the two of us from the southeast approached along the edge of a cornfield. It was only 5:30 A.M., pitch dark, and we had plenty of time to get in position. We proceeded slowly and quietly. No one had slammed a car door, and I couldn't hear any talking. So far so good. Thirty minutes later Gar and I were in place and beginning to set up the decoys. Hopefully, the other group was in position and quietly waiting for the appointed hour.

It has long been my view that in each of us resides a number of characters and behavior patterns. A man who is cautious and controlled in one stage of life is impulsive and even flagrant in another. My high-school biology teacher, Helen Field Watson, described this human fluidity in a wonderful poem entitled "Calculus" whose first stanza goes like this:

The gamut of man's desire
While sleeping and awake
In one day spans from ash to fire
From triumph to mistake.

Joe Shuster's life, which had been defined by one triumph after another, was about to become altered by one giant mistake. Where the day before he had been cautious and controlled, some unknown chemical cue was about to transform him into just such an impulsive, flagrant offender. Or, possibly it was the work of what Edgar Allan Poe referred to as *The Imp of the Perverse* in his essay by the same name, describing unwanted impulse. In this case, try as Joe might to prevent it, the unreasonable Imp gained control.

It was 6:15 A.M., exactly one hour before sunrise, and Joe was settled nicely into the reeds, hat on head, Coke-bottle glasses in place, when a lone coot paddled by his hiding place. A coot is a ubiquitous waterfowl, webbed feet and all, that isn't much of a flyer and requires considerable wing flapping and frantic paddling on top of the water before achieving lift-off. A coot attempting to fly resembles Charles Barkley's golf swing. It is not a pretty sight. Joe probably didn't even see the bird in the darkness, just heard its noisy paddling, and the Imp kicked in and he *shot*. Nine hundred and ninety-nine mallards woke from a sound sleep and erupted into the night sky. We couldn't see them, but that many wings beating frantically makes a sound you can never forget. They were all gone in a matter of seconds.

The geese really didn't want to leave. They understood the potential danger from the gunshot, but it was against their nature to fly in the darkness. They rose a few feet, then settled back on the water, then rose again, somehow caught a glimpse of the white decoys in the dark, and headed in our direction. Gar and I were standing in the decoys, some still in our hands, with a completely dumbfounded look on our faces. The geese approached, hovered over the decoys, wanting to land, but were disturbed by the two erect bipeds. We couldn't shoot; our shotguns were fifty yards away, and it wouldn't be legal for another half hour anyway. Finally, frustrated at being awakened and then kept from landing where they wanted, they disconsolately flew away in the darkness looking for a safer, saner environment.

Never in my long career as a hunting guide in Dickey County had I planned an excursion so carefully. Never had I positioned nine diverse individuals in close proximity to so many waterfowl. Never had so many birds escaped with only one ear-splitting shot being fired, and for that matter, never had a shot been fired so early in the day. Who did it? Who was the culprit? My first thought was of my son, Scott, who while not adverse to pulling the trigger a few minutes past sunset, had yet to shoot early. While not possessed of criminal intent in his teen years, Scott did harbor a relaxed attitude toward all rules and regulations. I remembered the conversation a few years before in the fog over on the James River with one of the guys from the office shouting out, "Scott, you're not supposed to shoot at birds on the river."

We all know how sound carries on a foggy morning, and Scott's reply came back loud and clear.

"It's O.K. I don't have a license anyway!"

He was twelve years of age at the time. But no, Scotty

wouldn't shoot an hour before sunrise. Neither would the Carlsons. It had to be Mast or Joe.

When it was light enough to see, Dick and I left our promontory and worked our way down to the slough. Our cohorts were standing at the edge of the water in a little circle around Joe. The Inquisition had begun, and like Galileo, Joe was beginning to wither under the questioning.

"Why did you shoot?"

"What were you thinking?"

"Don't you have a watch?"

"Did the bird attack you?"

"Let me see those glasses!"

"You can barely see in the daylight!"

"Have you no concern for your friends?"

That last question hit both Joe and me hard. I knew he would never intentionally cause discomfort for a friend. It was just a matter of being human and subject to our species's foibles and inconsistencies. Obviously, his normal rational façade had developed a fissure that cold, dark morning for reasons unknown even to Joe.

Later in the day, our trusty scouts informed us the mallards alone were back in Herman's at dusk, so the chalk talk that evening omitted any goose strategy. At the top of the board I had written in big block letters, "THE GUIDE SHOOTS FIRST." My diagram of the slough showed the six reliables, plus Garmaker, in their same position in the southwest corner and myself positioned (due to a strong south wind) at the north end of the slough. Joe was puzzled. "Where do you want me, Bill?"

I pointed to an *X* I had drawn about a half mile west of the water in the center of a plowed field.

"There's a rock pile here, Joe. You won't have any trouble finding it."

The ultimate banishment—but I felt Joe took it gracefully and even gratefully.

HERMAN'S SLOUGH

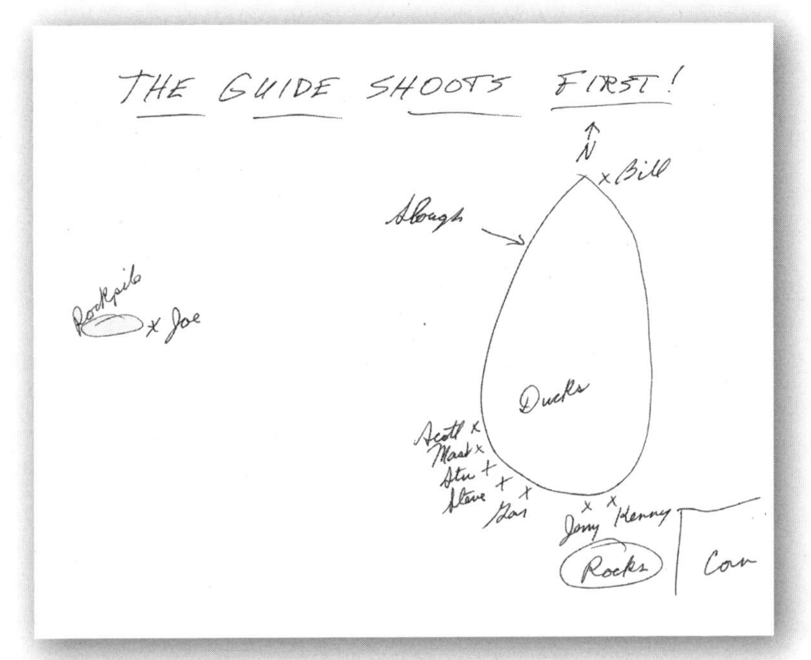

We left for Herman's only an hour before sunrise that next morning, without the goose decoys and with a much simpler strategy. We were all in place, including Joe in his rocky exile, just prior to shooting time. From my position at the north end of the slough I could barely make out the ducks at the other end, but the strong south wind was carrying their early morning chatter to me. I assumed they were getting prepared to leave, so rather than shoot, I shouted to my compatriots, "Shoot! Shoot! Shoot!" My voice evidently couldn't carry against the wind as there was no response. I shouted again as loudly as I could, "Shoot! Shoot! For God's sake, shoot!"

No response. It was now much lighter, but the boys hunkered down in the reeds, unfortunately, had taken my admonition to heart. They weren't going to shoot until the guide shot first. I didn't relish firing into the sky at nothing, but there was no choice. I shot. No response, either from ducks or hunters. The wind had carried the sound away. Now I was standing in the open, waving my arms and jumping as high into the air as my hip boots would allow. I shot again. No response. It was broad daylight now. Wouldn't you think someone would see me?

Finally the ducks did and they left, not to the south against the wind as we had expected, but to the east. All nine hundred and ninety-nine of them, gone in a few seconds. No one shot. The boys were still following instructions. The guide shoots first, and no one violated that rule for fear of banishment. That's the trouble with rules. There have to be understandable exceptions, and I had not allowed for that in my instructions. Another lesson learned in the practice of the art of guiding. I have been relieved over the years to never again have to deal with waterfowl in those numbers. It was obviously a situation we could not manage. We spent at least five hours in planning and execution, missed considerable sleep, and with a plethora of game within our grasp came away with one inedible coot.

A morning alone and a most unusual guiding error on my part had done wonders for Joe. His remorse, being an unnatural mantle for him to wear anyway, had completely disappeared. In its place, a defensive denial had begun to take form, tempered with a touch of belligerence. Since, due to the darkness, there were no eyewitnesses to his shooting, he argued that his accusers were basing their charges on audible evidence only. While we all know how difficult it can be to pinpoint the exact location of a particular sound, it is, however, fairly easy to locate a shotgun blast when you are standing only thirty feet away on a quiet morning. Regardless, the more he considered this line of reasoning, the more attracted he was to its validity. He was even heard to mutter something about "hiring an attorney" to clear his name, a practice he had engaged in previously in less-social contexts and with mixed results.

I was not surprised therefore to receive a letter from

Joe a week or so later. I seem to have misplaced that letter, which is unfortunate, as I doubt my memory after this period of time can do it justice. Joe's polemic traits were in full flower, and he had even gone so far as to couch the letter in legal jargon with many "whereases" and "stipulating" this and "stipulating" that. As I recall there were three basic themes to his argument. Number one, there was no empirical evidence, other than a loud bang, that he was the one who had pulled the trigger, which was an effort to blame someone, anyone, of his companions on that dark, cloudy morning. And number two, even if he was the culprit, there were extenuating circumstances, such as a miserable childhood, unknown genetic flaws, or stress caused by the guide's overly rigid instructions.

And lastly, because he had not been provided with a trial by a jury of his peers, his punishment was not only unjust, but also violated all the tenets of Anglo-Saxon law, and he was considering a lawsuit against the Guide. I believe there was even some mention of asking for the return of a set of dishes with the Sheraton Hotel *S* on the plates he had given the Carroll House a few years earlier. Joe had tried to pass those plates off as priceless antique family heirlooms, contending that the *S* stood for Shuster. In actual fact he had paid $10 for the set at a garage sale.

The letter was classic specious reasoning made even more absurd by its legalistic formatting. I viewed it as a pathetic attempt to somehow salve his conscience and his self-inflicted wounds and yet remain on good terms with the Perverse Imp. He, on the other hand, viewed his lengthy *mea culpa* as providing the ultimate absolution. Thirty-two years later this is still a subject of debate.

NINE

THE HORSE WRECK

In 1997, when I read about Baxter Black, the popular western writer and humorist, forming an organization called "Old Stove-up Cowboys of America," I realized there must be thousands of us OSC of A out there suffering in silence. Ever since my horse-wreck four years previously, I had been meaning to document the events of that day, but various forms of writer's block had prevented such catharsis. If the truth were known, I guess I just didn't want to admit being a party to such a stupid accident. But when I read Baxter Black's first few words, "If God were going to set up a situation where someone could get hurt..." I knew there was at least one soul who would comprehend and empathize with the confluence of characters that met in that alpine meadow on the Montana/Wyoming border on August 25, 1993. I would certainly conform to Baxter's definition of one of the characters involved. I'm bipedal, have a predatory ego, and sometimes at least have the judgment of an armadillo. My closest companion on that day was Red, a six-year-old, thirteen-hundred-pound gelding that I had ridden many times before without incident.

My friend, Joe Chenoweth, and I were going fishing at Lake Reno, high up in the Beartooth Mountains. Joe's ranch is located in the foothills of the Beartooth Range of the Rocky Mountains. The range only extends some fifty miles from the Stillwater River in southern Montana southeastward to the Clarks Fork of the Yellowstone River in northwestern Wyoming, but those fifty miles are arguably among the most scenic fifty miles in Montana. Many peaks in the range rise to more than twelve thousand feet, including Granite Peak (12,799 feet), the highest point in Montana. The Beartooth–Absaroka Wilderness, with its high plateaus, dwindling glaciers and alpine lakes, was our fishing destination.

Lake Reno is named after Major Marcus A. Reno, the highest-ranking officer next to George A. Custer at the battle of the Little Bighorn in 1876. Reno survived the battle and led his troopers with such skill that thirteen of his 140 men were awarded the Medal of Honor. He has a lake and a creek in Montana named after him. The impetuous Custer and over two hundred of his men did not survive, so he has a town and a national forest bearing his name. Reno Lake is located just a few miles from the northeast corner of Yellowstone Park, just a stone's throw from the southern border of Montana.

We'd have to drive with the horse trailer from Joe's ranch, through Red Lodge, Montana, and up over the Beartooth Pass on Highway 212 to get into Wyoming and come at the lake from the south. A sixty-mile, clockwise journey necessitated by the obvious lack of a direct route from the north over the Beartooths. The trip had been in the planning stages for only a week and was the result of Joe having acquired new, state-of-the-art plastic packs that fit snugly over the rigging of his mule's packsaddle. The mule, named Pebbles, certainly needed more exercise, but wasn't quite as eager as Joe to try out the new packs. Joe had retired the year before and, evidently, watching calves grow at his ranch near Roscoe, Montana, had some slack moments, at least in August.

I owned a quarter-section of Montana together with a cabin a few miles from Joe, and I was planning to fly up from Texas in mid-August, so the fishing expedition was planned around my visit. Most previous times I had visited Joe we moved cows or cleared brush, so this trip promised to be more in the way of a vacation. We would ride into the Beartooth–Absaroka Wilderness area on Wednesday, camp and fish for a few days, and come out on Sunday. Joe had all the gear and was anxious to see how Pebbles would handle the packs, and all I had to do was show up. This was the rationale offered in the phone call prior to my departure for Montana. Oh, and there were purported to be some enormous trout in those lakes.

Originally, we had intended to commence our trek, aside from the automotive phase, at the Island Lake Campground some five miles west of Beartooth Pass. Some acquired intelligence from some now-forgotten source had persuaded us that Lily Lake, some ten miles further west, was the place to disembark. On Wednesday, August 25, we arrived at the Lily Lake turnoff before noon, parked the horse trailer just off the road, unloaded, repacked the gear on Pebbles, saddled up Red, and set off up the trail. Low, scudding clouds crept past the treetops, promising a rain that never came, but not obscuring the "THIS IS GRIZZLY COUNTRY" sign. If you weren't aware of that fact before, the wording of the sign makes it pretty clear you're a trespasser without many rights.

Joe was walking, carrying a backpack, and leading Pebbles, while I, in deference to a bad left knee, was accorded the position of leadership, astride Red. For the most part it's an easy, uphill trail of maybe ten miles to Lake Reno, and if we'd both been riding we could have easily covered this distance in a couple of hours. As it was, we crested the trail into Elk Park, just above Lake Reno, at about 5:00 P.M.

Maybe it was the expanse of the meadow after the narrow trail, or maybe it was just a butterfly, but Big Red decided he had enough of my dismounting and mounting every few hundred yards to wait for Joe. He dismounted me permanently. With his first buck I lost the right stirrup, with his second, the left, and with the final twitch of his rear end, I became airborne. I can only estimate the height I attained before responding to gravity, but I could have sworn I caught a glimpse of the horse trailer some ten miles to the south. I landed awkwardly on my back, with my left elbow somehow pressed against my back, resulting in three broken ribs and a torn left rotator cuff. The ordeal had begun.

With much grunting, tooth-sucking, and ignoring the remonstrances of Joe to "stay down," I regained my feet. The impact had been considerable, producing, according to Joe, a sound similar to that of a sonic boom. I thought I had broken a rib but wasn't sure what other internal parts were ajar deep in my core. A ruptured spleen came to mind, although I wasn't exactly certain of its anatomical location. Joe was still cautioning me to stay down, but intuitively I understood my best position was upright and somehow moving downhill, back toward the horse trailer. We discussed our options: heading back now or waiting till morning. I couldn't climb back on Red, and there certainly wasn't time to walk out before dark. The decision was made for us by a passing wrangler named Bob, who rode into the meadow from the north, heading out. He reined up in front of my sagging and bedraggled form leaning against an equally bedraggled tree and greeted me with, "You don't look too good."

I've always admired the directness of Western people, but in this instance I could have used a nonjudgmental "howdy" rather than an opinion on my appearance. Bob was, however, most helpful. He was on his way back to his ranch, which was south of Highway 212 on the Clark's Fork River. He also knew how to get his Jeep within three miles of the meadow in which we were standing, because his nine-year-old son had been thrown from a horse and broken his arm in the same meadow just two weeks previously. Yes, if I could walk the three miles back down the trail to a spot where it forked he would meet us there at 8:00 P.M. with the Jeep.

We remembered the place and headed south almost immediately. At least I did. Joe had to gather Red and unload and tether Pebbles and, as there was no need to accompany me to the hospital once I was in the Jeep, Joe was returning to Elk Park to set up camp and fish the next day. After all, there was no point to acquiring new pack saddles to haul gear into a remote lake and then not go fishing. The logic seemed impeccable to Joe and I, but when Joe returned to his ranch a few days later his wife, Connie, upon learning I was still in the hospital in Cody, Wyoming, explained to him in no uncertain terms the error of his ways.

It was a slow trip down. If Red became bored on the way up, he literally ate his way down that mountain. I had acquired a walking stick to assist my amble, and with Joe walking and Red eating grass, we were a relaxed-looking trio. We did meet a pair of wranglers with packhorses heading north, and they also greeted me with that quaint Wyoming salutation, "You don't look too good."

We arrived at the appointed spot, a small, level clearing with a solitary pine in the center, a few minutes before 8:00. The shadows were long, and it would be dark shortly. Right on time, Bob came hurrying up the trail, not in his Jeep, but astride his heavily lathered horse. His Jeep wouldn't start, so he had called the Park County Sheriff, and the deputy was on his way in his Ford Bronco. Appropriately, I would transfer from one bronco to another. He was proceeding up a dry creek bed, and it would be slow going, but the odds were looking better that I would get out that night. An ambulance from Cody had also been ordered and would be waiting for us at the trailhead. The walk down had tired me considerably, and I limped over to lean against the pine tree.

Joe had tied Red to a large clump of sagebrush, and he and Bob were quietly talking. A full moon had risen over our little clearing and the temperature was dropping quickly. September was only a few days away, and the evening air reminded us of that. At that point, Red decided to move to a slightly better patch of grass. I couldn't believe he was still eating. The rope stretched taut against the sage clump so Red, with a toss of his head, pulled the clump out of the ground. Somehow he managed to get the hitching rope down under his chest and under his belly so the sage clump, still tied at the end, just cleared his back feet. When he walked faster to get away from the brush it would bounce higher and strike him higher on the back of his legs.

He was soon proceeding at a full gallop with the rope under his belly and the brush bouncing just high enough to smite him right under the tail. He was agitated and moving fast, circling our clearing. Joe and Bob were now aware of his bizarre dance and started yelling at Red. They managed to change his direction so that now he included my tree in his route. Every time he galloped by the saddle horn knocked another branch from the tree. Soon I would be leaning in bright moonlight against a defoliated tree, a stump no less. Big Red had me in his sights and was going to get me before the deputy arrived.

Then, just as abruptly, he veered north through the

trees and headed back to Elk Park and Pebbles. Heaving a large sigh and muttering under his breath, Bob vaulted onto his horse and sped up the hill after Red. I received the definite impression he was sorry fate had sent him through that meadow earlier that afternoon. Forty-five minutes later he returned with Red in tow, sans sagebrush, and we settled down to continue to wait the arrival of the Bronco.

Sometime after 10:00 P.M., as I was starting to lose track of time, headlights from the Bronco began to appear through the trees, coming up the creek bed. Soon help arrived in the person of Deputy Dan Estes and a lady paramedic whose name I can't recall, which was the first thing she asked me to recall, my name. An article in the *Billings Gazette,* describing the incident a few days later, referred to me as "an injured Texas man," but said that my name "wasn't available." I don't recall ever offering my nationality, but I certainly remember the lady's first question as she stood in front of me, pad and pencil poised, "Now, *what* is your name?" From her tone I thought possibly I was to be arrested for wandering around in "GRIZZLY COUNTRY," but I did give my name.

She noted that my blood pressure was high and my aspiration slight, and after ascending the rocky creek bed, she felt certain that one or both of my lungs would be punctured by descending over the same route. Joe argued philosophically that it was either go down by Bronco or plant me there. Hearing those options, I climbed into the right front seat of the vehicle and let the argument roll. We were now connected via radio with a doctor in Cody whose logic must have prevailed: "Drive carefully and get him out of there."

I rolled open the window, said "adios" to Joe, who promised to visit me in the hospital when he finished fishing, locked my right arm over the door to cushion the bumps, and off we went, down towards the trailhead. They tell me it was only six miles, more direct than the trail, but it took three hours. Dan drove perfectly: he crawled that Ford over boulders and never created a ripple. The cold air from the open window and my vise grip on the door helped me stay awake. It was a beautiful night, clear and bright from the harvest moon. It was such a lovely night to be outside that when we arrived at our destination there were about thirty people standing around, their pickups lined up behind Joe's horse trailer. They had evidently heard news of the wreck on their CBs and had come to see if this anonymous Texan was coming out horizontally or vertically.

Actually, I was kind of in-between. After three hours of clutching the door of the Bronco, my right arm seemed a detached appendage that I couldn't straighten, while the pain in my left shoulder and back caused me to tilt sixty degrees in that direction, so as I was peeled from the vehicle I think I did a fairly accurate imitation of Quasimodo, the Hunchback of Notre Dame. I can still see the onlookers' eyes peering intently at me as I was assisted onto the gurney, either amateur physicians attempting to evaluate my condition or just bored locals with nothing better to do at 1:00 A.M. I hadn't realized there were that many people in the neighborhood.

I seem to recall there were two ambulances waiting. Maybe they thought I was in two pieces, but they loaded me into one and we set off for Cody. After Dan's careful ministrations clambering over the rocks in the creek bed, I wasn't quite prepared for the flight into Cody. Those of you who have traveled over the Sunlight Basin Road know there are a fair number of switchbacks, but we made the seventy-mile trip in an hour and a half. What made the drive even more thrilling was that the young driver drove with his left hand, his right shoulder draped over the seat and his head turned to the rear of the ambulance where he carried on an animated conversation with one of the two nurses overseeing my care.

When we arrived at the hospital it was after 2:00 A.M., and the only area that was lighted was the emergency room. There waiting for me was the ER doctor, a tall, morose, mustachioed gent wearing cowboy boots and jeans secured with a silver belt-buckle the size of a saucer, resembling for all the world a large-animal veterinarian. I just couldn't resist asking him the name of the medical school he had attended. Just to be sure, you know.

I was astounded at the scope and quality of the equipment they had in their emergency room. CT scanning devices, X-rays, ultrasound and MRI equipment, all brand-new. When I commented on such an impressive display, the doctor proudly informed me that they received all the "horse wrecks" from the park, which I understood to mean that several dudes each year suffered from some sort of equine catastrophe in Yellowstone Park. I spent a week in the hospital with a surgeon assigned to my case in the event my spleen was ruptured. The care I received was first-rate; everyone was concerned, professional, and extremely considerate. If you ever have a horse wreck in Park County, Wyoming, let me recommend the West Park Hospital in Cody. It's well worth your stay.

On Sunday, which was the day we were supposed to return from our fishing trip to the Lazy JC, I decided to call Patricia to advise her of the accident and my location and perhaps garner a little sympathy for my plight. Her response was, "Oh, you and that Joe! You're always getting into some trouble with him! If you think I'm flying to Cody, Wyoming, to help you get home, you're very mistaken! You got there by yourself, and you can get home by yourself." Obviously, she was most upset with me and also with Joe, as was his wife, Connie.

When I was discharged on the following Wednesday, Joe drove down from his ranch to Cody to take me to the airport, and I learned there were no big trout in those mountain lakes, only tiny ones not worth catching, but Pebbles loved the new packs, so the trip hadn't been in vain.

I won't bore you with my inability to secure a wheelchair or hail a riding cart at the Denver airport, necessitating a long, slow shuffle through the terminal which resulted in missing my flight to Dallas. The only pleasant part of the ensuing wait was meeting Baxter Black in the Admiral's Club and having a discussion about horse wrecks. Now that I think about it, maybe I was his inspiration for forming the Old Stove-up Cowboys of America.

Big Red died the following winter. Joe said it was colic, but I'm certain it was remorse.

TEN

THANKS FOR THE WORST HANGOVER I EVER HAD

I was going through the old Guest Log for the Carroll House a few days back and came across this notation dated October 4, 1986, from my nephew, David M.: "Thanks for the worst hangover I ever had." As my son, Bill, had discovered the missing log and returned it to me a few weeks earlier, I called him to ask if he had noticed

David's comment. Bill had not, but in the course of our subsequent conversation he remembered and refreshed my memory with a few other instances of overindulgence he had observed through the years. As we chuckled over our recollections I realized that my memoirs would not be complete without at least some discussion of the possible relationship between hunting trips and drinking.

In the past forty years we have probably entertained over three hundred guests at the Carroll House on October weekends. A small percentage of those people, certainly less than five percent, have experienced unpleasant results from the rural hospitality dispensed at Bee's Bar and its successor, the Ranch House. I have always been surprised and sometimes dismayed by the individuals who fell prey to John Barleycorn, and I have long tossed this issue around in my mind looking for a rational answer. One conclusion I have come to was perhaps best expressed by Samuel Johnson, who was quoted in Boswell's *Life of Samuel Johnson* almost 250 years ago as saying, "A sober man who happens to occasionally get drunk, readily enough goes into a new company, which a man who is drinking should never do. Such a man is without skill in inebriation."

Old Sam Johnson hit the nail right on the head there. None of the characters we're going to discuss in this chapter possessed any "skills in inebriation." That being the case, my next puzzlement revolves around the "why" of their behavior. I hesitate to invoke Poe's Perverse Imp theory again, although that might possibly be a contributing factor at some point in the inebriation process. Each individual case is as different, as the individuals are obviously different, and I'm certain behavioral scientists have carefully studied the phenomenon. Not having access to any of these studies, I have necessarily formulated my own hypothesis and offer it to you by way of these two case studies.

Jerry C. was a forty-five-year-old direct report of mine in our Minneapolis office. He had previously been a property underwriter at Chubb and as such harbored a passion for details and minutiae and was definitely your administrative type. He was of high value to me, as administering anything was not my strong suit. I much preferred the style of pointing out the direction I wanted to go and trusting that everyone was following me. Jerry's job was to make sure they did. He was neither a hunter nor much of an outdoorsman, except for an occasional round of golf. When I invited him for a weekend of duck hunting at the Carroll House he responded in the affirmative, as he did to all of my suggestions, but in his eyes I thought I glimpsed a brief initial hesitation.

A native Bostonian, Jerry had lived in the Midwest only a few years and, except for a quick sally to Mount Rushmore the previous summer, was not at all familiar with the Dakotas. We traveled together in my station wagon with my two boys and Murph, the Lab, along good old Minnesota Highway 55. I pointed out the many things of interest along the way: the ever-declining vegetation, the flatness of the Red River Valley, the many potholes in North Dakota, the Benedictine convent in Hankinson, North Dakota, the sharp, unexpected ninety-degree turns in the road, and the hundreds of ducks zipping back and forth. He seemed impressed, but perhaps he wasn't. The boys had memorized the names of all thirty-three towns between Golden Valley, Minnesota, and Fullerton and recited them over and over as a sort of mantra—as a way of entertaining our guest and breaking the monotony of a five-hour drive at top speed on a two-lane road.

There was a large crowd at the Carroll House that weekend, mostly guys from the office and a couple of insurance company executives we were trying to get to know on a different basis rather than as supplicants. In those days business relationships were extremely personal, so the better you knew someone and the more experiences you had shared with them, the easier it was to do business. I remember one of the underwriters present was from the Insurance Company of North America (INA) headquarters in Philadelphia, Pennsylvania, and our weekend together completely changed our dealings for the better.

After our traditional supper of lasagna, all ten of us trooped down to Bee's Bar to savor the Fullerton nightlife and renew acquaintances with the regulars. As I was always the first to bed because of my breakfast responsibilities, I always felt myself fortunate to miss the final few hours of frivolity before Bee closed the doors. During that critical period, for whatever reason—the excited anticipation of the next morning's hunt, the significant cultural difference between a big-city watering hole and Bee's Bar, or just the change in elevation—Jerry C. exceeded his normal liquor ration by a significant amount.

I didn't become aware of his distressed condition until I was frying bacon and eggs for everyone the next morning. Well, not everyone. My two boys would have bacon but no eggs, as I hadn't brought enough eggs for all. They weren't at all pleased about this decision when I told them and even less so some ten minutes later when Scott sidled up to me and quietly said, "Thanks a lot, Dad. Mr. C. just threw up his breakfast." Scott's point being that I had wasted his eggs on a queasy delinquent. It was obvious that a hearty breakfast would not remedy Jerry's hangover, but I had another sure cure in mind. Strenuous physical exercise, such as a quarter-mile crawl over plowed ground with a shotgun cradled in your arms, seemed to produce positive results for most sufferers.

I don't really have an excuse for what happened next, other than I blew the call, as umpires and guides sometimes do. In the early morning scuffle of getting my charges out the door and into their vehicles, making sure they had the necessary equipment, and then staging them at various locations around the slough, I somehow deposited Jerry a half mile away from the slough rather than the expected quarter mile. His instructions were to crawl to the northeast, keeping the slight pink in the eastern sky to his right. I had that part right. It was a dry but blustery morning with considerable dust blowing, not ideal for crawling on your belly, shotgun in tow, and with your nose six inches above the plowing. Jerry was nothing if not obedient, however, and off he started in the dusty dark.

Maybe forty-five minutes later, those of us at the edge of the slough heard what we thought initially was the yelp of a wounded goose. It wasn't completely daylight yet, and the sound seemed to be coming from the southwest, in the direction of our crawler, and seemed to be some distance from us. As we focused on the sound it gradually became clear it was not a goose in distress, but rather a human being with some serious hiccups. I left my position and headed across the plowing in the direction of our troubled friend. I found him, still a quarter of a mile from his destination and still crawling, although the intermittent yet massive hiccups he was experiencing were convulsing his body in such a manner that his crawling motion was more like that of a giant caterpillar inching along.

"Jerry, stand up! I'm sorry I started you in the wrong place. Are you all right?" I asked. He stood shakily, a sweaty apparition covered with dirt. He appeared disoriented and was unable to speak for a minute or two. Then he blurted, "I kept crawling. I was afraid if I stopped the dust would cover me up and you'd never find me."

Those of you who have undergone basic training in the Army or Marine Corps are well aware of the rigor attached to crawling with a rifle over a one-hundred-yard course. By the time I reached him, Jerry had crawled over a quarter mile, some four hundred yards across plowed ground with dirt clumps the size of footballs to navigate—an amazing feat and one not to be attempted unless you are suffering from a serious hangover which has completely destroyed that section of your brain responsible for self-preservation. The effort had left him exhausted but sober, so I drove him back to the Carroll House where he slept the rest of the day. Refreshed but subdued by dinnertime, he quietly responded to the many solicitors inquiring about his health, a completely changed man from the night before thanks to the salubrious effect of a good crawl.

We shall now turn to the story of David M., the instigator of these recollections, who memorialized his transgressions by mentioning them in the Guest Log. At the time, David was in his final year of law school at the University of Minnesota, avidly learning the lucrative practice of suing people and corporations for exemplary and punitive damages.

He and my son, Scott, were only a few months apart in age and were very close, as cousins often are. There was one period in their lives when they conversed exclusively in dialogue lifted from movies they had seen. Their quick wits and recall of various phrases uttered in *Monty Python and the Holy Grail* or Mel Brooks's *Young Frankenstein* delighted them to no end. Their conversations were unintelligible to me as I, of course, had never seen the movies. On this particular weekend they had travelled to the Carroll House together, bringing with them their youthful insouciance and buoyancy.

As my good friend Tom Reed was also in camp that weekend, we were treated to some excellent Margaux wine he had brought back from France. It enhanced our standard lasagna dinner considerably. Evidently the two cousins had never encountered such a velvety concoction in their early experimentations with alcoholic beverages. This was not the Gallo offering favored by college students. They enjoyed Tom's contribution immensely and grew more animated and voluble as the dinner progressed, particularly David, who was talkative by nature.

We followed our established pattern and after dinner adjourned to the Ranch House for our annual conclave with our local friends. I was making phone calls to arrange entry into some hunting land for the morning and did not accompany the group, so from this point on I can only provide secondhand reports as to the ensuing events. I can however, imagine the scene as the two ebullient youngsters greeted their friends in the bar. At this point Scott had been coming to Fullerton for fifteen years and was well thought of by the locals. This was only David's second trip, but everyone remembered him as a personable, interesting character who laughed easily and was very much at home in a bar environment. He also harbored the admirable trait of being able to hold his liquor. Even if he had one drink too many—in his case the third drink—his demeanor changed only slightly, and some said for the better in that he became very quiet. At the same time, a rather beatific, glazed smile appeared on his face and he resembled the most reflective of monks.

It would be instructive here to recall the admonition of Samuel Johnson regarding "going into a new company, which a man who is drinking should never do." David was in "a new company" quite different from his fellow law students, and under the influence of the Margaux he decided to lecture the assembled farmers, truck drivers, and elevator workers on the obvious benefits of *Nuclear Disarmament*. This was a somewhat abstract but topical subject to be discussing in a North Dakota bar on a Friday night during harvest season. You may recall that in 1986 the Soviet Union, led by Mikhail Gorbachev, and the United States, with Ronald Reagan as president, were beginning to negotiate the removal and destruction of various classes of weapons systems that the two nations had deployed in Europe. The Intermediate-Range Nuclear Forces Treaty (INF) was signed the following year, much to the dismay of the right-wing zealots in each country and the palpable relief of the rest of us.

According to Scott, David was in full law-school mode, using all of the Socratic method he had been taught to convince his audience of the advantages of dealing with the Soviets. The locals, however, were for the most part suspicious of the "Russkies" and weren't accepting his well-crafted argument, a difficult response for David to accept. Part of their rationale was a perverse mindset that generated considerable pride in the fact that North Dakota was home to most of our Intercontinental Ballistic Missiles (ICBMs). Hundreds of these nuclear weapons were housed in missile silos scattered throughout the state and targeted for all of the major cities in the Soviet Union. Pride wouldn't be much defense however, as David pointed out, if the Russkies launched a preemptive strike on the missile silos. The collateral damage from such a strike would most certainly include even the Ranch House. Surely his audience could see the disadvantages of that loss.

While the patrons weren't buying David's position, they were, however, buying him drinks to fuel his ever more passionate reasoning. They were enjoying the moment even if the kid from the Cities didn't know what he was talking about. Eventually the alcohol conquered his exhortations, and David grew silent. The monk-like smile appeared on his flushed face, and with no one taking the affirmative position the discussion died. People wandered out to their pickups and went home. Scott assisted David back to the Carroll House, his fervor for better US–Soviet relations completely forgotten. I'm sorry I missed the show.

Of course there was no mention of this heated discussion the next morning, and it also follows that I would be the last to be informed that the cousins had overindulged. That's another defining characteristic of people without skill in inebriation: their memories are trained to adopt a most selective process whereby the night before either didn't happen, or as David's entry in the Guest Log implies, their host was responsible for their actions. Sadly, such is the human condition.

My considered analysis of the actions of these two individuals, one a callow Midwestern youth and the other a mature New Englander, actually eliminates even a tenuous connection between hunting and drinking. Rather, my conclusion is that their behavior stemmed from a significant change from their normal environment, coupled with the excitement of the glamorous Fullerton nightlife and the stimulus of a scintillating conversation with their intellectual superiors. Behavior modification in these circumstances is not unusual. It happens to people at high-energy parties in New York, San Francisco, and Rome every weekend. It has nothing to do with hunting. I'm glad we cleared that up.

ELEVEN

SUR-FOOT

For over sixty years, I've been a bird hunter, upland and migratory. I've chased geese from Hudson Bay to Chihuahua and ducks from the potholes of Saskatchewan to the shallow, saline mashes of Culiacan, Mexico. Annual expeditions to the Dakotas after pheasants and periodic ramblings in west Texas after the elusive quail have been a constant in my life. While I've ranged north to south for thirty-five hundred miles, my east–west wanderings have been restricted to the five hundred miles between the 95th to 105th meridians west—a true Midwesterner.

Growing up in South Dakota, I don't think I ever knew anyone who hunted deer. Pheasants were our game. And after moving to Minnesota, I never felt the urge to enter the woods with a million armed Scandinavians who had spent the previous night gulping substantial amounts of aquavit in deer camp. On the other hand, my friend Joe Chenoweth had been raised in Montana hunting four-legged creatures and since retiring had supplemented his beef diet with venison, elk, and moose on a regular basis. So, for the past few years, at Joe's urging, I had applied in February, unsuccessfully, for a big-game license in Montana. License-less, I had followed Joe as an observer and companion on several hunting forays on his ranch, the Lazy JC.

In April of 1996, however, a letter arrived from the Montana Department of Fish, Wildlife & Parks stating, "Congratulations! A Montana Big Game Hunting License is enclosed." Opening day was set for Sunday, October 27th, and I immediately called Joe to advise him of my good fortune. Six months later, on Friday, October 25th, accompanied by big-game hunters from all over the United States, I flew into Billings, Montana. I sat next to a Chevy dealer from North Carolina, and he and the lady on the window talked nonstop during the two-hour flight while I read the paper and inadvertently learned a great deal about their lives. There was a very low ceiling at Billings, which was an indication of the weather to come.

Joe was waiting at the airport, and we happily bumped into Liz Somers, our old neighbor, who was meeting someone arriving on a Delta flight. First stop was for lunch at a corner café near the Chenoweth's new townhouse on 17th Street, quick inspection of said town-house, then off to Fox to pick up the Jeep, which was being repaired. Driving down U.S. Highway 212 toward Red Lodge and the Beartooth Pass it started to rain, then sleet, then snow as we neared Fox. I was assigned to drive the Jeep, and we needed four-wheel drive as we left Fox. It was snowing more heavily now, and the visibility was fading as we neared the Luther turnoff.

It snowed all night, and by 7:00 A.M. on Saturday morning we had thirty-six inches of powder snow and it was still coming down. Joe and I spent most of the day shoveling and blowing snow. Because it was a light powder, it was the first time I'd actually seen a snow-blower work effectively. Most of what we were doing was for the animals: paths to feed the horses, paths for the dogs, although Buster certainly didn't need help. He bounded quite nicely. By midafternoon, the storm abated and a doe and yearling appeared from the southeast. Only the doe's back, the yearling's head, and the top strand of the barbed-wire fence were visible above the snow. Joe and I watched some football in the afternoon, but I can't remember who was playing.

The weather forecast for the next day was for colder temperature with strong winds. It didn't bode well for opening day. We were resigned to crowding two bulky bodies into the cab of the tractor and driving down the driveway the two miles to the county road. That's assuming we could get the tractor started. After dinner, Keith Clark from Roscoe called about coming up in the morning and bringing his son Rusty, who had a cow permit and Sur-Foot, his handmade hunting vehicle.

It had required considerable imagination and craftsmanship on Keith's part to blend the following disparate parts into a functioning vehicle: the body was a 1928 Hudson Super Built four-door sedan, the frame a 1974 three-quarter-ton Ford 4x4, the engine a 1974 360 Ford V8, the transfer case as well as the differentials were a 1945 Chevy two-ton, the steering and suspension were a 1974 three-quarter-ton Ford, and the fuel tank a 1951 International 9 1949 Studebaker. The winch was a WARN 8,000 pounds, the heater a Twin Fan from a school bus, the instrument panel a 1966 Dodge half-ton pickup, and the seats from a 1979 Ford van. The end result was, according to Keith, "a real 4x4 that won't fall apart and will climb a tree if the bark don't slip!"

We awoke to partly cloudy skies and fifteen degrees, but fortunately no wind. If Sur-Foot could navigate the road up to the Lazy JC, we had a chance to get out after the wily elk. We worried, however, whether they would be moving around in all this snow, particularly if we were the only hunters in this neck of the woods. We were ready to go at 6:30, which was sunup, but no sign of Keith and the estimable vehicle. They came plowing up the driveway around 7:00 A.M., Sur-Foot pushing waves of snow in front of an eighteen-inch bumper/cow catcher with a significant winch mounted in the center. It was an all-terrain, all-weather vehicle, and without it we might as well have been inside watching Bob Dole on *Meet the Press.*

Keith Clark, master welder and cabin builder, sported greasy tan overalls, a plaid shirt, the black wool cap favored by the local ranchers in winter, dark glasses, and a full gray beard; he seemed all in one piece and confident ol' Sur-Foot could navigate the approaches to Butcher Mountain. Rusty, a quiet nineteen-year-old freshman at Montana State, wore tan coveralls covered with a blaze-orange vest, a red stocking cap, and inadequate boots. He'd left his good boots at a friend's house the night before and reputedly had been bowling in Red Lodge until 3:00 that morning. None of us older gents realized bowling alleys stayed open till 3:00 A.M., but when you're nineteen, I guess anything is possible. I was sporting my blaze-orange parka complete with hood and resembled nothing less than the Great Pumpkin of cartoon fame.

After introducing me to the Clarks and getting our

rifles, we climbed—and I use the verb most specifically, as it was a three-foot jump to the running board, with hand grips assisting the leverage—into Sur-Foot. With a small cooler on the floor, a lunch pack jammed behind the seat, and rifles between our knees, we set out for the Forest Service land which meant driving though a mile of the Lazy JC, then across a piece of the Switchback Ranch, altogether about three and a half miles southeast of the ranch and all uphill through three to four feet of snow. As it turned out we needn't have packed ourselves in so snugly, because we hadn't traveled a hundred yards to the east when Joe yelled, "There they are!"

And there indeed were a herd of twenty-five to thirty elk just over the brow of the hill, maybe two hundred yards below us. You can imagine the activity. Keith, with more experience dismounting Sur-Foot, was first out and loaded, down on one knee in the snow and firing. Joe was cussing about not being loaded and was fumbling through his pockets looking for shells. Rusty was the second one firing and hit one of the cows. I was third into the action after locating my shells in the left-hand pocket of my jacket—great if you're left-handed. The elk were moving up the hill to the south now with the biggest bull bringing up the rear, three hundred yards away, but not running, maybe because of the snow. I was concentrating on him not only because he was the biggest, but also the closest. Four shots in succession, fired from a standing position to the left of Keith, without any effect at all. Keith was cussing now, exclaiming, "I'm not that bad a shot, boys," although nothing had fallen. Joe finally got off a couple of shots from the right side, and it was over; they were out of range and cresting the hill, and we had missed them all save one cow who was limping and straggling behind.

Now, how much time has this fusillade taken? We fired at least fifteen or sixteen shots at the bunch and they didn't actually break into a run 'til near the end. One to two minutes maximum, but you don't think about time when so much activity and excitement is being compressed into such a small sliver. I wonder if Einstein had a formula for stationary time.

As we clambered back into Sur-Foot, Joe remarked in his laconic fashion, "This wasn't the first time I haven't been ready when we've seen elk on opening day." The same must have been true for the animals. They were as surprised as we were by the sudden encounter, which explains why they hadn't bolted over the hill immediately. Well, plenty of time for the postmortem later. The issue at the moment was to run down the cow that had been hit. She wasn't hard to find. While the other animals had breasted the hill, then crossed the thin creek before entering the aspens, she appeared to our right, moving fast on three legs and giving no indication how badly she was hit. She followed the tracks of the herd, but after crossing the creek turned left into a scraggly group of aspen. She was obviously having trouble plowing through the snow. We found her a half hour later and after field dressing winched her uphill through the aspens and dragged her back to Joe's ranch. I don't know how we would have gotten her out without the winch attached to Sur-Foot's front bumper.

Joe decided the best way to chase the elk was to drive over to his neighbor's place and approach them from the northeast, which we proceeded to do, only a forty-five-minute trip. There were more people chasing these elk than we realized. Joe's neighbor had three friends on snowmobiles and two on horseback who had watched our earlier encounter and subsequent barrage through binoculars with a mixture of amazement and disbelief. The horseback riders were slogging away somewhere in the Forest Service, but the machine people were hanging around the Forest Service's gate, waiting for the snow to pack down, which it does, somewhat to our dismay. Ol' Sur-Foot could navigate the earlier powder pretty well, but the wetter condition bogged him down at least on an uphill run. So Joe and Rusty decided to hoof it, a decision they would regret over the next two hours. Plodding uphill through three feet of snow is hot, tiring work.

Keith and I drove downhill to the county road, then back uphill to Joe's ranch. We had decided to drive the tractor as a backup for Sur-Foot in case we couldn't get up that one incline just above the Forest Service gate.

Good plan, poor execution. Willard, the mule, had bitten through the electric cable leading to the engine heater of the tractor, which wouldn't (couldn't) start. How Willard survived chomping through a 210-volt hot cord is anyone's guess. It must have melted his fillings.

The storm had moved on, and it was a bright blue sky now; the white snow was gleaming as we retraced our path from the morning across the creek and into the Forest Service. Now that the snow was settling you could discern a slight depression in the snow where our tracks had gone before. We stopped, then turned east toward Joe and Rusty and stopped again to listen and to shout for them. They should be coming by now. No sound other than the echo of "Joe," "Joe." Deciding we were too high, we turned around and started down toward the fence line marking the Forest Service boundary. Just as we reached the gate, two cow elk trotted in from the right across the meadow in front of us, and shortly after the rest of the herd came trotting in single file into the meadow, the bulls in the rear and the biggest bull on the other side of the cows, using them very effectively as a shield.

Keith and I tumbled out of the vehicle and stood at the posts on either side of the gate, searching through our scopes for a legal bull. Keith hit one and yelled, "I've got one down." My scope flitted between the head of the big bull—not a realistic shot—and the shoulder of another who had actually reversed his direction and was now headed back to the east from whence they came. I shot, and missed, snow spurting at his feet. I had shot beneath him on a slightly downhill trajectory. Keith then fired over his head, and the bulletproof bull was gone along with all his associates.

Once we reached his downed animal, Keith's first act was to notify his wife of his accomplishment via his cell phone. The people at Motorola probably never anticipated this particular use for their equipment. "Honey, I'm up here on Butcher Mountain, and you'll never guess what's happened! I just shot a five-point bull elk!" Obviously, this wasn't an everyday occurrence, even for an experienced hunter.

Keith field dressed the bull, a significant animal weighing close to a thousand pounds, while I tromped along the path of the fleeing herd following a faint blood trail that eventually stopped. We'd hit another elk, but not seriously. We returned to the fence line and spotted Joe and Rusty coming down the hill, tired but happy to see us and to learn their trek hadn't been in vain. They had obviously driven the herd back to the west. We later learned the elk had continued west toward the East Rosebud River where Joe's neighbor and his group, once they realized the elk were moving in that direction, had driven ahead to intercept them and bagged two big bulls.

During our post-hunt analysis that afternoon Joe came to the conclusion that my rifle, a Browning 30.06, was not properly sighted. The storm the previous day had prevented us from following the basic rule of making certain your gun's sights are properly aligned. He was right; the rifle was shooting about *three feet low.* I was fortunate I hadn't shot my toes off.

TWELVE

THE ART OF GUIDING

Like most other learning experiences, the Art of Guiding is best mastered by committing mistakes. Mistakes or errors in judgment are effective learning tools that have defined our development from the Garden of Eden to Bernie Madoff. The problem is, of course, that most of this wisdom, accumulated over thousands of years, doesn't automatically transfer from one generation to the next.

Two-year-olds, for instance, only learn that fire can burn you by touching something hot. A duck hunter can only learn how far to lead a flying bird by shooting at the first duck in line and having the last in line fall, as I did during my first duck-hunting experience. I suppose there are schools or seminars you can attend to learn about hunting, but I can't recall hearing of any such nonsense when I was growing up in South Dakota. We learned by doing. In the 1940s, everyone I knew hunted pheasants. Out-of-state hunters, whom I didn't know, visited our town every fall to hunt the long-tailed birds. As they came by the thousands, it was a great economic boon to the state, and it still is thanks to a concerted advertising campaign.

The South Dakota style of hunting is to arrange twenty or twenty-five hunters in a more or less straight line and march them through a cornfield or across the soil bank. "Soil bank" is the antiquated term for what is now more elegantly called the Conservation Reserve Program, or CRP, a government program that pays farmers to remove land from cultivation and return it to its natural state, i.e., native grasses. There are all sorts of rules and regulations, as you might expect, but that's the basic idea. The program creates a marvelous habitat for all sorts of animals and birds, but particularly deer and pheasants.

I really never enjoyed the South Dakota style of linear hunting, for while it does keep the birds from running around you, it also is a recipe for disaster with twenty or so city dudes with loaded shotguns. My friends and I preferred to hunt in groups of two or three on late Sunday afternoon, after the crowds of hunters had dispersed the birds into small swales of grass that were easier to surround. We all had single-shot shotguns, which required you to take fairly careful aim as you were only going to get one shot at the bird. Maybe time has dimmed my memory, but I believe I was a better wing shot at age sixteen than I am today, probably due to that single-shot weapon. Not surprisingly, my reaction time today is quite a bit slower as well.

Aside from sporadic pheasant hunts in southern Minnesota during my college years, I didn't have much opportunity or time to hunt during the fifteen-year period between 1950 and 1965, when Van and I decided to go to Saskatchewan for a week. Previous chapters have dealt with our detour to Dickey County, North Dakota, and the ensuing forty-five years of hunting in that grand locale. The early years, which could be labeled the *Goose Years* because of our fascination with, yet misunderstanding of goose behavior patterns, were mostly years of experimentation. As neither of us had hunted geese before, many of our early attempts to outsmart them were pathetically unproductive. A couple of experiments come to mind that while embarrassing to recall do serve to emphasize our willingness to try anything.

Our first and perhaps our most unique peccadillo

occurred during our second visit to Dickey County in 1966. It involved attempting to sneak up on feeding geese, also known as "goose spooking" because such an attempt is almost certainly guaranteed to fail. We came upon perhaps two hundred snow geese feeding in a small, pasture-like field that also contained one lone, grazing horse. Novices that we were, our first maneuver was to crawl on our bellies toward the birds, slowly and carefully across the short grass. The geese ignored our approach until we were almost within shotgun range, say seventy-five yards; they then flew away with much agitated honking and squawking. We arose and retreated to the edge of the field. The birds circled a time or two and then settled back into their breakfast area. We shrugged, dropped to the prone position again, and started another crawl, only this time from a different direction, but with the same result. We slithered to within seventy-five yards, and they left again with even more honking and squawking. We arose and walked over to the fence line to review our strategy while they circled the field and again settled back in, this time very close to the horse as though seeking his protection, which gave Van an idea:

"Those birds aren't afraid of that horse, so why don't we disguise ourselves as a horse and walk right up to them?" When an idea such as this springs from the brain of a man known for his acumen and rationality, who could possibly refuse to accept it? Besides, at this point I was willing to try anything other than another crawl, although I was at a loss as to what materials we had on hand to effect a horse disguise. We really needed a full-body mount similar to the ones used in vaudeville. As it turned out we only had a five-by-three-foot piecc of cardboard that served as a temporary liner in the back of the truck. This one-dimensional rectangle would have to do for the horse's body. We obviously had four legs between us, which generated an intense discussion as to which pair of legs would support the anterior portion of the horse. I won the coin toss and became the horse's front half and Van, well, you know.

My position was much easier as I only had to bend my back a little, hold the top of the cardboard with one hand, and hide my shotgun behind the cardboard with the other. Poor Van had to walk with his back bent at ninety degrees to hide his upper body behind the cardboard, hold its bottom edge, and hold his gun out behind him to represent a most rudimentary tail. We convinced ourselves that if we could maintain a side view of our silhouette to the geese, we might be able to fool them until we walked close enough for a shot. The biggest deficiency of our disguise was the size and roundness of my head. I really needed a much longer nose and more erect ears.

Assuming our awkward positions, we set off in a nonconfrontational diagonal line towards the feeding geese, always keeping the cardboard side of our ersatz horse turned toward the birds. We meandered slowly, with Van suffering considerable agony from his bent position but gamely portraying his role as the posterior end of the horse. Perhaps from a distance of three or four hundred yards our silhouette might have been, if not a horse, most certainly that of a four-legged animal. From a distance of seventy-five yards we evidently resembled two guys carrying a piece of cardboard, as the geese again hoisted themselves into the air and flew away, this time for good. The real horse never looked up from his grazing.

In the critique that followed, Van—once he was able to stand erect—apologized for concocting such an unpractical and unseemly approach, while my remonstrances only dealt with the deficiencies of my stubby nose and flat ears. Which prompted Van to pronounce, "Well, that only proves it's easier for a guy to act like a horse's butt than it is to impersonate his head." A quote for the Ages.

The next year we brought goose decoys, full-bodied ones of course. No more silhouettes for us of any type. I should add that the most effective method I ever found to attract birds to your decoys is to play a recording of live geese landing in the decoys. We tried that once in Chihuahua, Mexico, with outstanding results, but learned later the method is illegal, even in Mexico. That's another important guiding lesson; try to stay within the law.

This next judgmental error is even more difficult for me to recount, as it involved the welfare of my boys, Billy and Scott. It happened a year or two after the horse incident, when we were still in our experimental stage. In those days, there were fewer geese, so you could only hunt them until 1:00 P.M. The three of us were cruising the countryside at about 12:30 P.M. when we spotted a flock on the ground a half mile or so north of the Oakes Road. Further examination showed there was an east–west prairie road that appeared to lead right to their location. A prairie road is defined as a set of tire tracks across the prairie between two agricultural fields. This particular path, when approached from the east, would keep us hidden from the geese. If the road contained no serious badger holes beneath the grass, we should be able to drive the station wagon at a fairly good clip, burst over the last little rise, and be in their midst before they knew what had happened.

The decision was made, but time was of the essence. It was now 12:45 and counting. I told my sons to stand on the dropped tailgate with their loaded shotguns in hand and hold on tight. I would accelerate as much as I could to the geese, then slam on the brakes when I reached them, and the boys would jump off the back and fire away. As Billy was age twelve and Scott age ten, they eagerly bought into the plan. Riding on the tailgate across the prairie at thirty miles per hour was right up their alley. Our dog, Mandy, didn't appear too pleased with the idea, as the open back door was certain to bring considerable dust into her area.

It was now 12:50 and time to go. I shoved down on the accelerator and away we went: ten, fifteen, twenty-five, then thirty miles per hour, dust streaming behind us. When we crested what I thought was the last undulation or rise in the ground, there before us were not geese, but instead a gigantic rock pile at least ten feet in height and covering the entire road. These rock piles are a feature of the landscape in eastern North Dakota, the rocks having been deposited by the glaciers and removed from the earth by generations of farmers and left in piles in the fields. In New England the rocks were arranged as fences, but as North Dakota had no need for fences, they end up in piles.

Let me say that being confronted by rocks rather than geese came as a serious shock to all of us. I slammed on the brakes, resulting in the two boys and their guns flying off the tailgate in opposite directions. Fortunately, we were on a downslope, so their fall was cushioned somewhat, but it was frightening nonetheless. Mandy slid over both the back and front seats and was deposited on the floorboard next to me. The skidding tires raised an intense cloud of dust and that, accompanied by the screeching brakes, caused our prey, just over the next rise, to leave the area, again with much squawking and honking. Oh well, it was past shooting time anyway.

The boys picked themselves up, dusted themselves off, retrieved their guns, which fortunately hadn't fired, and approached the vehicle. Billy stood by my open window, looked me in the eye, and asked, "Well, Dad, do you have any more bright ideas?" The ultimate put-down, and I deserved it for putting my boys in harm's way in order to save some time—a very bad decision. On the way back to the Carroll House I cautioned the boys about mentioning the incident to anyone in town, as I didn't want Mrs. Sturma to get wind of it. She would for certain report me to the Child Abuse Authority.

After a decade or so of sometimes-successful strategies you slowly learn what techniques work for what species of prey. You learn how to dig goose pits in the solid North Dakota earth, how to arrange duck decoys to take advantage of the wind, which is a constant, and how to proceed slowly, oh so slowly, in thick pheasant cover. Gradually, over time, you acquire enough knowledge to feel you are qualified to advise and direct other hunters. In other words, to pass yourself off as a guide.

The epiphany comes when a group is congregated around you in the pre-dawn light, looking at you for direction, and you answer their questioning gaze with firm, resolute instructions. "Okay, we'll spread out here about forty feet apart and walk to the south, against the wind. Stay in line, although you, Charley, on the end you can get out maybe ten yards in front of the line. Walk slowly; this isn't a race, and zigzag a bit back and forth. Let the dogs work and pay attention to them. When a pheasant is hit, run to the spot it landed to help the dogs. Sometimes these dead birds get up like Lazarus and are able to run away. Never shoot at a bird on the ground; there may be a dog nearby. And try not to shoot each other! We'll start out when it's light enough to tell the difference between a hen and a rooster. Good hunting!"

At that moment you've taken the field marshal's baton out of your duffle and grasped it in your hand. You have designated yourself as the guide and can no longer afford to make the mistakes you made when you were just experimenting. One error in judgment and you lose credibility and the confidence of your fellow hunters. In my later years, as a good executive should, I have turned the guiding responsibilities over to my son, Scott. When I informed him of this one evening at the Ranch House, it was astounding to observe his transformation. Normally, Scott would enjoy the social aspects of an evening with his Fullerton friends with little concern about the morrow. After receiving the baton, his casual conversations ceased and he began networking with the farmers, asking good questions about pothole locations, prairie roads, landmarks, and permission to hunt on their lands. Such are the responsibilities of the guide, and I'm pleased to say he adapted quickly. He had obviously learned from his father's mistakes.

Reflecting back to that transitional moment, I realize at that point I exchanged my field marshal's baton for the shaman's rattle. I am no longer the *Head Guide* but the

Chief Storyteller. As we gather in the living room of the Carroll House after the day's hunt, one of the younger members of the group will ask, "Did you really live in a tent when you first came up here? Where was your campsite?" Those questions will generate the "Tenting on the Prairie" story, which only I can tell because I am the only survivor. My partner, Van, passed away three years ago on his ninety-seventh trip around the sun. His struggles with the collapsing tent and various misadventures hunting geese stood him in good stead when he encountered the vicissitudes of old age.

Then someone else will suggest, "Tell the story about the Frenchman," and I will recite for all to hear the sad but heartwarming tale of Jacques and the Wintergreen Skoal. My son, Bill, usually assists with the telling of this story by describing in scathing detail the shortcomings of my 1976 Scout that took Jacques and me to Aberdeen to catch his plane. Another evening the discussion will turn to the various strategies to hunt geese and that will, of course, call for a recital of the ever-popular Horse Masquerade escapade.

In true shaman fashion, I usually only respond to questions from my congregation unless a specific incident that occurred that day opens the possibility of a learning lesson for them. This is particularly applicable when the lesson might help them to improve and overcome some errors in judgment. This inexorably leads us back to the tragic story of Joe Shuster and the unwanted impulse, which has instructive benefits for all the listeners.

The conclusion we have reached in our October discussions is that it is important to create a narrative when attempting to explain human behavior. The summation of our shared knowledge is that there are no definitive answers, only *stories*. We would have it no other way.

PHOTOGRAPHS

CHAPTER ONE: This photo of myself, my son Billy, age nine, and Taffy was taken in October of 1967. We are standing in front of the home-made Quonset hut.

CHAPTER TWO: This is an aerial view of Fullerton, North Dakota. The Carroll House is obscured by the grain elevators.

CHAPTER THREE: This picture of the remodeled Carroll House was taken in the Fall of 1987.

CHAPTER SIX: This was taken in September of 1970 at Sitting Bull's grave site at Standing Rock reservation in Fort Yates North Dakota. The black Lab is Mandy.

CHAPTER SEVEN: "The White Dogs of Kaska" in September of 1968. Back row: David Burkholder, D'Arcy Leck, Bill Baker, and Joe Shuster. Front row: Bob Bartholemay, John Sagehorn, and Dick Garmaker.

CHAPTER ELEVEN: Keith Clark and Sur-Foot of Roscoe, Montana. The photo was taken on October 27, 1996 at the Lazy JC ranch.

ILLUSTRATIONS

CHAPTER FOUR: This depicts Tom Reed's broken-field run toward our goose pit; just prior to his sudden disappearance.

CHAPTER FIVE: This illustration shows Jacques on the morning after the Wintergreen Skoal incident. He is waiting for me to drive him to the airport.

CHAPTER EIGHT: This relates to the activity on page 91 where I am attempting to get the attention of my friends at the south end of the slough.

CHAPTER NINE: The artist's rendering of the wrong way to dismount a horse.

CHAPTER TEN: This scene relates to the discussion on nuclear disarmament outlined on page 118.

CHAPTER TWELVE: An example of our early attempts to out smart geese, as described on page 137.